IRISH SOCIAL SERVICES

IRISH SOCIAL SERVICES

JOHN CURRY

SECOND EDITION

INSTITUTE OF PUBLIC ADMINISTRATION

First published 1980
Second edition 1993
Reprinted 1994

Institute of Public Administration
57-61 Lansdowne Road
Dublin 4
Ireland

ISBN 1 872002 07 2
(ISBN 0 902173 97 9 first edition)

British Library Cataloguing-in-Publication Data

A catalogue record for this book is available
from the British Library.

Cover design by Butler Claffey Design, Dún Laoghaire
Typeset in 11/12 Baskerville by Phototype-Set Ltd., Dublin
Printed by Colour Books, Dublin

Contents

Tables

Figures

Preface to Second Edition

Justifying an introductory book on services which affect practically every household in Irish society and the very livelihood of many of them presents little difficulty. Until recently the availability of published material on housing, income maintenance, education and health services was rather limited. During the past decade or so this situation has been rectified with the publication of various books, reports and articles on individual social services or aspects thereof. It is still essential, however, to have a publication which contains a broad overview of these services. This book is intended to serve that purpose and it should be of interest not only to students of social administration but also to anyone concerned with how the basic social needs and problems are catered for. Hence the purpose of this book is to provide an introduction to the evolution, nature and scope of the key social services in Ireland.

Revising this book some twelve years on is challenging and it presents its problems. Inevitably, some omissions are unavoidable because of the sheer scope of the areas covered. There is the added problem that in treating the subject matter as comprehensively yet as concisely as possible, some topics are not given the emphasis some readers might like. Certain issues can be pursued in greater depth with the aid of the bibliography. How to write a book that remains relevant and topical for a reasonable period on services which inherently are subject to constant change is yet another dilemma. In this context statistics used throughout are meant to indicate either trends or the situation at a given time and they can be updated by reference to the sources. Every effort has been made to include the most recent relevant information and the main developments since the first edition was published in 1980.

   This book is based on lectures for the Bachelor of Arts in Public Management and the National Certificate in Public Management at the Institute of Public Administration. I am therefore indebted to those students who, unwittingly, have been of inestimable help in constantly clarifying issues and justifying the relevance of the subject matter. My special thanks to IPA staff Anne Kelly who cheerfully typed several drafts and Finbarr O'Shea for his painstaking editing.

   While many have helped in various ways towards the publication of this book none of them are responsible for any views or errors contained therein.

John Curry
January 1993

1

Introduction

The social services are the main instruments of social policy and are those which are provided by the state and other agencies to improve individual and community welfare. The main social services are income maintenance, housing, education, health and welfare or personal social services. Before considering the general relevance of these services in Irish society it is useful to examine the background against which social services developed and the broad objectives behind the services.

What is social policy?
Donnison, in a report for the National Economic and Social Council (NESC), defined social policy as:

> Those actions of government which deliberately or accidentally affect the distribution of resources, status, opportunities and life chances among social groups and categories of people within the country and thus help to shape the general character and equity of its social relations.[1]

By this definition it could be argued that virtually all government policies or programmes have some implications for the well-being of the population. Consequently all government programmes could be assessed in terms of their contribution to the achievement of national social objectives. Certain public programmes, specifically those of income maintenance, housing, education and health, have traditionally come to be regarded as the main constituent elements of social policy since they are the most visible instruments of achieving the distributive aims of government. In addition to these public programmes there are others, such as fiscal (e.g. taxation) and occupational (e.g. benefits relating to a particular employment) measures, which could also be included since they too provide benefits for individuals and the community at large. The primary focus of this book, however, is on the five main social service areas outlined, i.e. income maintenance, housing, education, health and welfare services.

The NESC has indicated that government intervention by means of social policy is a response to the following four factors:

- A socially acceptable distribution of income and other resources could not be guaranteed by a market economy, i.e. one in which the state does not intervene. A market economy would not, for example, guarantee an income to those unable to earn a living in the labour market. In any case the distribution of incomes guaranteed in the market may be the result of many factors, some of which are accidental and have little to do with equity.

- A socially desirable level of provision of some particular goods and services and their consumption by different groups will not necessarily be achieved through the market. For example, the attainment of certain levels of education and the utilisation of health care services confer benefits not only on the individual but also on the community in general. If left to market forces alone the utilisation of certain services would be less than optimal since many would not be in a position to afford them.

- The states of dependency in which people may find themselves, such as unemployment or illness, are social risks which are a hazard for the entire community and are not necessarily due to individual shortcomings. Governments can ensure, through appropriate social policy measures, that the burden of dependency is shared by the community as a whole.

- The concept of citizenship in countries has evolved from a purely legal status of belonging to a particular country to one which confers rights to participation in the well-being of the community, including social services provided as an expression of social solidarity.[2]

Over several decades, intervention by governments in developed countries has increased in relation to social policy. More recently, constraints on public expenditure have led to a questioning of the effectiveness and efficiency of various social programmes and to consequent cutbacks.

Aims of social policy

If the above are the main factors accounting for government intervention in the social area, the precise objectives of such intervention are not always clarified. This is certainly true of Ireland. In the absence of explicit objectives, Kennedy examined various official sources to determine what the aims of social policy were in post-war Ireland.[3] She concluded that three main aims were discernible:

- the relief of poverty and the provision of a minimum standard of living for all
- equalisation of opportunity
- increased productivity and economic growth.

These, according to Kennedy, could be described as the humanitarian, egalitarian and economic aims of social policy respectively.

In 1981 the NESC outlined what it considered to be the aims of social policy.[4] These were as follows:

- the reduction in inequalities of income and wealth by transferring resources to those in need and by equitably distributing the burden of such support
- the elimination of inequalities of opportunity which arise from inherited social and economic differences
- the provision of employment for those seeking work
- the provision of access for all, irrespective of income, to certain specified services
- the development of services which make provision for particular disadvantaged groups in the community
- the development of responsible citizenship based on an explicit recognition of the network of mutual obligations in the community.

Interestingly, these aims were referred to, though not necessarily endorsed, by the Fine Gael/Labour coalition government of 1982-87 in its national plan, *Building on Reality.*[5]

With the exception of the provision of employment the aims as outlined by the NESC are being met to a greater or lesser degree. The extent to which they are being achieved will be referred to, as appropriate, in the following chapters.

Importance and relevance of social services

There are several reasons why the social services are an integral part of Irish society. These include utilisation of the services and the level of public expenditure on them.

The social services are availed of by practically everyone in Irish society. Over one-third of the population are in receipt of weekly income maintenance payments and at some stage the members of every household avail themselves of a scheme or schemes administered by the Department of Social Welfare. Just over one-quarter of the population is engaged in full-time education. Most of the housing stock has been either provided or subsidised by the state. While one-third of the population has entitlement to the full range of health services approximately one in every seven persons is treated in hospitals annually.

Just under half of government current expenditure is spent on the social services (Table 1.1) with income maintenance accounting for the highest share of the four social service areas. It should be noted that there is no separate budgetary provision covering welfare or personal social services since these services are provided for under other headings. It should also be noted that expenditure on housing is the area most subject to fluctuation depending on the demand for housing and other factors.

For the general public therefore the social services can be vitally important, with some people dependent on them for their very livelihood. For government, the social services are a commitment to society, accounting for a considerable proportion of public expenditure which, especially in recent years, has come to require constant monitoring.

Factors influencing social service provision

In most countries social service provision will have evolved

Table 1.1: Government expenditure on social services, 1988-1991

Social services	Expenditure, £m (current prices)				As % of government expenditure			
	1988	1989	1990	1991(p)	1988	1989	1990	1991(p)
Current Expenditure								
Education	1,073	1,142	1,206	1,200	13.4	14.2	14.3	13.2
Health	1,001	1,070	1,197	1,346	12.5	13.3	14.2	14.8
Housing	32	24	13	8	0.4	0.3	0.2	0.1
Social Welfare								
(i) Social Ins. Fund	1,095	1,159	1,346	1,388	–	–	–	–
(ii) Exchequer	1,606	1,585	1,546	1,798	20.1	19.7	18.3	19.8
Total (Excl. Social Ins. Fund)	3,712	3,821	3,962	4,352	46.4	47.5	47.0	47.9
Capital Expenditure								
Education	61	54	67	62	4.6	3.9	4.1	3.7
Health	44	48	46	42	3.3	3.5	2.8	2.5
Housing	202	136	122	124	15.1	9.8	7.4	7.4
Total	307	238	235	228	23.0	17.2	14.3	13.6

Source: Estimates 1992, Reports of the Department of Social Welfare 1989-1991, Department of Finance
(p) Provisional

over a period of time. Coughlan has summed up the situation as follows:

> Most people are aware of the *ad hoc* and fragmentary way in which the social services came into being; they were largely a piecemeal growth, introduced at different times to cover different categories of need and in response to different pressures, the result of a wide variety of motives – humanitarianism, social idealism, political expediency, the desire to damp down social discontent, the response to the spread of democracy and universal suffrage, the need to provide an environment conducive to industrial development. Seldom were they the expression of a coherent philosophical outlook.[6]

While broadly similar social services exist in most developed countries there are considerable differences in emphasis, the type of services provided and the priorities given to certain services. Thus, in relation to health services, for example, the extent to which free services are available to all or part of the population can vary greatly.

In Ireland, the development of the social services has also been piecemeal, as the following chapters will illustrate. Developments normally occur for a variety of reasons, in response to needs and demands, with the government having regard to cost considerations.

Once governments decide to provide social services, various factors come into play to influence the shape, the precise nature and the future development of the services. A number of key factors have been identified which determine the type and level of services provided in any country.[7] These include socio-demographic, economic and ideological factors. In examining the development of Irish social policy a number of factors are briefly examined. It should be stressed, however, that it is the interplay of all these factors which is important rather than the primacy of any one in particular.

Socio-demographic factors
It is axiomatic that changes in the total population and changes in the composition of the population will determine or influence certain priorities. Thus, very simply, whether the population is increasing or declining will have

implications for social services in general but for education and housing in particular. In the 1950s when emigration was running at an annual average of 40,000 it was deemed that housing demand had been virtually met and consequently housing output declined (see Chapter 3). Within a decade, however, the situation had been reversed – the population increased for the first time since the 1840s, emigration declined steadily, the demand for housing increased and housing output rose.

Apart from trends in the total population, provision of services is also influenced by changes in the birth rate and life expectancy. Increases or decreases in the birth rate have obvious implications for child care services, educational facilities and income maintenance payments and allowances for children. One of the notable features of the demographic situation in Ireland in the recent past has been the steady decline in the birth rate from a peak of 22.8 per 1,000 population in 1971 to 15.0 in 1991. The actual number of births fell from 74,400 in 1980 to 52,690 in 1991 (a decline of 29 per cent). This fall in the birth rate has already had an impact on enrolment in first level education and will work its way through the second level system. Life expectancy has increased throughout this century and this has implications for the provision of pensions as well as health and welfare services for the elderly.

Over the past two decades there has been a dramatic change in the age structure of the population (Table 1.2). One of the features has been the decline in the young population (under 19 years) due to the sharp decline in the birth rate. By contrast, the number of people in the prime working age group (25-44 years) has increased by over 50 per cent. While the number in the 45-64 year age group has changed marginally, the number of elderly persons has increased steadily. The age dependency ratio (the ratio between the working age groups, i.e. ages 15-64 and the groups aged under 15 and over 64) has fallen from 100:74 in 1971 to 100:62 in 1991. This ratio indicates the relative burden of providing services which benefit the young and old. Those in the working age group have to bear the burden, through direct or indirect taxation, of providing services for the dependent groups. The real burden of dependency, i.e. the ratio between those actually at work and others, is much greater. In 1991 it was 100:214, and this has been exacerbated by the steady rise in unemployment.

Table 1.2: Age structure of population, 1971-1991

	Age groups						
	0-14	*15-19*	*20-24*	*25-44*	*45-64*	*65+*	*Total*
1971							
Number (000s)	931	268	215	626	608	330	2,978
Percentage	31.3	9.0	7.2	21.0	20.4	11.1	100.0
1981							
Number (000s)	1,044	326	276	838	591	369	3,444
Percentage	30.3	9.5	8.0	24.3	17.2	10.7	100.0
1991							
Number (000s)	963	333	265	949	618	395	3,523
Percentage	27.3	9.5	7.5	26.9	17.6	11.2	100.0

Source: Census of Population

The distribution of population between urban and rural areas and the density of population also has important implications for the social services. It is less costly per unit, for example, to provide certain services such as water supply in high density urban areas than in sparsely populated rural areas. Specialised services such as hospitals are usually located in the larger urban areas, making access difficult for those living in remote rural areas. Approximately three-fifths of the population in Ireland live in urban areas (towns with 1,500 persons or more). Many rural areas contain dis-proportionate numbers of elderly persons, a legacy mainly of persistent and selective migration. This has implications for the provision of services for the elderly.

Economic factors
The level of state investment in social service provision is influenced by the financial resources available. In a period of economic growth it is likely that developments and expansion of social services will occur. By contrast, when there is little or no economic growth the aim may well be to retain, if not reduce, the existing level of services. Kennedy

has outlined different social policy phases, both expansionary and regressive, in Ireland between the end of World War II and the mid-1970s.[8] Thus the 1950s was a period of relative economic stagnation with few developments in the social service area. By contrast, the period from the mid-1960s to the early 1970s was one of economic growth accompanied by a series of developments across the social services.

Economic growth, however, does not necessarily result in increased employment. One of the features of the Irish economy over the past few decades has been the continuing rise in unemployment. The average annual number on the live register of unemployment rose from 70,300 in 1974 to 109,000 in 1977 to 254,000 in 1991. The rise in unemployment not only means a drop in revenue to the state through taxes, but also an increase in state expenditure on income support schemes for the unemployed and their families. The substantial increase over the past two decades in the population in receipt of social welfare payments is largely accounted for by the rise in unemployment (see Chapter 2). The NESC in one of its most recent comprehensive reports identified the creation of employment and the consequent reduction of unemployment and involuntary emigration as primary objectives in the strategic issues for the 1990s.[9]

Party political factors
While party political ideology may have influenced the shape of social service provision in other countries, its impact in Ireland has not been significant. In general there are no fundamental differences between the political parties on matters of social policy. This is not to deny that there has been different emphasis given to developments, or priorities to others, depending on the party or parties in power. What is obvious, however, is that there is a broad continuity in relation to social policy irrespective of the parties or combination of parties in government. There has not been any major social policy development which an opposition party or parties may have criticised while the necessary legislation was being passed but which they have been prepared to undo on gaining power themselves. All too frequently, however, there has been opposition of a politically opportunistic nature, involving point scoring, rather than the principled type. A classic example is

afforded by the family planning legislation introduced in 1978 by the Fianna Fáil government to allow for the availability of contraceptives, hitherto banned. In 1985 the Fine Gael/Labour coalition government amended the 1978 Act in order to make contraceptives more readily available. This was opposed by Fianna Fáil, the then main opposition party. Yet, ironically, in 1991/92 Fianna Fáil, by then in government in coalition with the Progressive Democrats, was in a position to liberalise the law further (albeit against a background of an increase in AIDS) in order to make contraceptives even more widely available.

It would be difficult to describe any of the Irish political parties as having strong ideologies in relation to social policy. Most tend to be pragmatic and to reflect the attitudes of the population towards social service provision in general and to specific developments required. There is broad support among the population at large for services provided either directly by the state or by other agencies with state assistance.

While the differences in ideology between parties may be negligible, individual politicians have made significant contributions to the development of social services. An example is the late Donogh O'Malley who as Minister for Education was responsible for introducing free post-primary education in 1967, several years before it was planned to be introduced and without sufficient reference to the cost implications from the viewpoint of the Department of Finance. Without his unorthodox initiative, it has been asserted, it is unlikely that free post-primary education in its present form would ever have been introduced.[10] In this way, Donogh O'Malley made a far greater impact during his short term as Minister for Education than many of his predecessors or successors.

The role of the Catholic Church

Until relatively recently, one of the more notable features of Irish society has been the pre-eminence of Catholic social teaching. In the past this emphasised the principle of subsidiarity, i.e. that the state should not undertake functions which could be fulfilled by individuals on their own or by the local community, and that the state's role should be to supplement not to supplant. The debate over the proposed Mother and Child Scheme in the late 1940s illustrated the importance of this issue (see Chapter 5). Since Vatican Council II (1962-65), the Catholic Church has been concerning itself increasingly with inadequacies in social policy and social provision. It has been urging the introduction of measures designed not simply to ameliorate the effects of disadvantage and poverty in society but also the removal of the cause of these problems. This renewed emphasis on social issues by the Catholic Church has been exemplified by the sentiments expressed in the hierarchy's pastoral, *The Work of Justice* (1977), and several reports by the Council for Social Welfare (a sub-committee of the Catholic hierarchy). The Conference of Major Religious Superiors has also been to the forefront since the mid-1980s, not only in highlighting issues of social concern but also in proposing alternative policies.

Vocational and lobby groups
The influence of vocational and lobby groups should not be ignored in the development of social service provision in Ireland. In some countries trade unions have had a formative influence on social service developments. In Ireland their role has probably been more limited but significant nonetheless. While the primary concern of trade unions has been the remuneration and general working conditions of their members, as one of the main social partners they have been to the forefront in pressing for reforms. The National Understandings between government, employers and trade unions in the early 1980s followed a period of national wage agreements and contained a number of commitments related to social policy. More recently, the unions have had a significant input in the *Programme for National Recovery* (1987) and the *Programme for Economic and Social Progress* (1991). These two documents (agreed between government and the social partners) contain extensive and detailed commitments to social policy developments. Their inclusion is attributable largely to the influence of the trade union movement.

Many voluntary bodies involved in providing services also have a lobby role and frequently press for changes in the areas under their remit. Some of these have representative umbrella organisations which perform this particular function on behalf of their members. Lobbying usually takes place in advance of proposed legislation and, more commonly, in the form of pre-budget submissions.

Historical and external influences

The foundations of many existing social services in Ireland were laid by British governments before independence had been achieved in the 1920s. Examples of early state intervention in various social services include primary education (1831), children's services (1908), non-contributory pensions (1908), unemployment and sickness benefits (1911).

The influence of the Poor Law, which came into effect in Ireland in 1838, on the development of social services must also be stressed. It was out of the Poor Law, for example, that the public hospital system developed. The initial central feature of the Poor Law was the workhouse which was designed for the very destitute. The philosophy of the Poor Law was based on the concept of less eligibility, i.e. the conditions of persons within the workhouse should be less eligible than those of the lowest paid worker outside. While many of the workhouses, the visible signs and reminders of the mid-nineteenth-century Poor Law, were demolished and remodelled for other purposes after independence, some of the services which the Poor Law spawned remained until the 1970s. These include the dispensary system, replaced by the choice-of-doctor scheme, and home assistance, replaced by the supplementary welfare allowance scheme.

The British influence continued long after independence. The contiguity of Britain and the free flow of labour between the two countries (mostly one-way, to Britain) inevitably meant that comparisons would be made between the social services in each country. Consequently, there was a general tendency to look to Britain as the first reference point when a new scheme or development was being considered. Not infrequently, modified versions of schemes already in existence in Britain have been introduced in Ireland.

While it can be difficult to make general comparisons between the social services in different countries, it appears that over the past few decades differences in the range and quality of services between Northern Ireland and the Republic have narrowed. By 1990, a comparative study of the social security systems in Northern Ireland and the Republic could indicate that:

> ... the same contingencies are catered for under both systems and, taken overall, the differences are not substantial.[11]

It is at least arguable that this has been the result of a continuous and conscious process to remove some of the obvious or perceived obstacles to the eventual unity of the two parts of Ireland. Ireland's entry to the European Community in 1973 also had an impact on social service provision. If nothing else it served to heighten comparisons between Ireland and other member states and to provide wider reference points than heretofore. The EC influence has been of a direct and indirect nature. The direct influence has been exemplified by EC directives, such as the directive in 1978 on the equal treatment of men and women in matters of social security. The indirect influence is more difficult to determine but it is nonetheless important. While it was never the intention of the EC to secure uniformity in social service provision, obvious gaps in social security coverage, for example, became apparent from the time Ireland became a member. The publication of a discussion document by the Department of Social Welfare on *Social Insurance for the Self-Employed* in 1978 was undoubtedly influenced by the fact that Ireland was the only EC country which did not extend social insurance cover to the self-employed.

Recent interest in social policy
Over the past few decades there has been increased interest in social policy in Ireland. This is reflected in the output of publications dealing with social services and social issues in general. Several of these have helped to create and increase public awareness of social issues. Reference must first be made, however, to an early pioneering work – a paper entitled *Social Security* read by Dr Dignan, Bishop of Clonfert and Chairman of the National Health Insurance Society, to the management committee of the Society in 1944. In his paper Dr Dignan outlined what at the time appeared to be radical proposals for reform of the Irish social security system.

It is only since the mid-1960s that various publications containing analysis of the various social services began to emerge in Ireland. These works include Coughlan's *Aims of Social Policy* (1966), the various publications of Kaim-Caudle in the 1960s and early 1970s, especially *Social Policy in the Irish Republic* (1967), Ó Cinnéide's *A Law for the Poor* (1970), and 'The Extent of Poverty in Ireland' (1972) by the same author.

The publications of several agencies and institutions have also contributed to the debate on social services. At one level governments have commissioned reports on the various aspects of the social services, e.g. *Report of the Commission of Inquiry into Mental Illness* (1966), *Investment in Education* (1965), *Report on the Industrial and Reformatory School System* (1970), *Report of the Commission on Social Welfare* (1986), and *Report of the Commission on Health Funding* (1989).

At another level various advisory and research agencies have been established and through their publications have contributed to the growing debate on social issues. In 1973 the National Economic and Social Council was established, its main task being 'to provide a forum for discussion on the principles relating to the efficient development of the national economy and the achievement of social justice and to advise the government on their application'. The reports of the NESC, as well as being invaluable sources of information, have raised important social policy issues and have contributed to a continuing debate on social problems and policies. The same could be said of many publications emanating from the Economic and Social Research Institute (ESRI), e.g. the report by Professor Dale Tussing on *Irish Educational Expenditures – Past, Present and Future* (1978). Similarly, the work of the Combat Poverty Agency, a statutory body established in 1986, which succeeded the non-statutory National Committee on Pilot Schemes to Combat Poverty (1974-80), has highlighted the extent and nature of poverty in Irish society.

The above illustrate the growing interest in and concern with social policy in Ireland and the need to assess the impact of the social services. This is in marked contrast to the situation several decades ago when the same services were rarely subjected to any serious debate or analysis.

The focus of this book will be to examine each of the social services, with reference to their origin, how they are financed and administered, and some of the key issues of concern.

2

Income Maintenance

Introduction

In this chapter the term 'income maintenance' is used to describe the system of cash payments made to people who experience certain contingencies, such as unemployment and sickness. This system is more popularly referred to in Ireland as 'social welfare' and that terminology is derived from the fact that it is the Department of Social Welfare which is responsible for the administration of the vast majority of the cash payments (and some benefits in kind). The term 'social welfare', however, may have a much broader meaning in other countries. It should also be noted that in many other countries the term 'social security' is used to describe the system of cash payments and, additionally, in some, eligibility for health services.

The basic purpose of an income maintenance system is to provide income support for people who, for whatever reason, experience a loss of income or whose existing income is regarded as being insufficient. In this context it is useful to make a broad distinction between those in the labour market and those outside it. Examples of those in the labour market who experience an income loss would be the unemployed and the short-term ill, while the retired and chronically ill are examples of those outside the labour market.

Over several decades, the types of income contingencies catered for have become accepted in most industrialised countries. They include unemployment, retirement, widowhood and invalidity. It is not unusual, however, for countries to have special measures for other categories. This is certainly true of Ireland where special schemes have been developed for deserted wives and unmarried mothers.

Types of income maintenance schemes

There are three main types of income maintenance schemes: social insurance, social assistance (means tested) and universal.

The distinguishing feature of social insurance schemes is that eligibility is determined on the basis of social insurance contributions paid. They are financed by compulsory contributions from employers and employees. Once the contribution conditions are satisfied there is an intrinsic entitlement to benefit irrespective of any other income the person may have.

In the case of social assistance or means tested schemes on the other hand, eligibility is determined by an assessment of means. Only if the means are below the threshold set for the particular scheme will the claimant be entitled to a payment. Partial rather than maximum payment will be paid where the means are greater than the minimum floor set (zero income in some schemes). In general, claimants of social assistance will have either no social insurance contribution record or a broken social insurance record, which effectively disqualifies them from social insurance payments. Means tested schemes are financed from general taxation.

Under a universal scheme there are neither social insurance contribution conditions nor a means test and a payment is made without respect to income. The most important universal scheme in Ireland is that of child benefit, payable in respect of all children up to a specified age.

The Irish income maintenance system embraces the three types of schemes referred to above. For some time the trend has been to extend the social insurance base and the social insurance schemes account for the larger share of expenditure. Nonetheless the social assistance schemes are likely to be an important element of the system for many decades to come. Social insurance and social assistance schemes are referred to as contributory and non-contributory schemes respectively. This is because of the way in which they are funded. In many instances there are complementary social insurance and social assistance schemes. Thus, for example, there are widow's and old age contributory pensions for those who satisfy the contribution conditions, while on the social assistance side there are widow's and old age non-contributory pensions for those who do not satisfy the contribution conditions and who qualify on the basis of a means test. The payments under social insurance are invariably higher than those for social assistance although the difference is not consistent across schemes.

Evolution of income maintenance system

The income maintenance system evolved over several decades. Schemes were introduced at different times in response to different needs and due to different factors.

An outline of the chronological development of the main income maintenance schemes is given in Figure 2.1. This is not meant to be comprehensive but simply indicates the piecemeal nature of the development of the system.

Since the background to the development of the income maintenance schemes is given elsewhere[1] only a broad outline is presented here.

The Poor Law system of the nineteenth century (of which the workhouse was the central feature) did not originate as a system of income support, nor was it ever intended by its founders to be such. Due to various circumstances, however, it reluctantly became involved in this area. At the beginning of this century, the only resort of those on low incomes was to the Poor Law. Gradually reliance on the Poor Law, of which a main remnant from the 1920s onwards was the discretionary system of home assistance, was diminished as schemes were introduced for different categories of claimants.

The first categorical scheme of income maintenance was the old age non-contributory pension which came into effect in 1909 following the passing of the Old Age Pension Act the previous year in Westminster. Since then, the various schemes for other categories have been introduced, as Figure 2.1 illustrates. It is interesting to note that the complementary old age contributory pension was not introduced until 1961. There is no particular pattern to the way in which the various schemes were introduced. There were particular circumstances surrounding the introduction of each scheme. It should be obvious from Figure 2.1, at the very least, that the development of the system was not planned in a coherent manner. At best it can be

Figure 2.1: Chronological development of main social welfare schemes

Date	Insurance schemes	Assistance schemes	Other schemes
1838			Poor Law
1909		Old age pension	
1911	Unemployment benefit Sickness benefit		
1920		Blind pension	
1933		Unemployment assistance	
1935	Widow's and orphan's pensions	Widow's and orphan's pensions	
1942			Cheap fuel scheme
1944			Children's allowance Cheap footwear
1947	Department of Social Welfare established		
1961	Old age pension		
1966		Smallholder's assistance	
1967	Occupational injuries		Free travel Electricity allowance
1968			Free TV licence
1970	Retirement pension Invalidity pension	Deserted wife's allowance	
1973	Deserted wife's benefit	Unmarried mother's allowance	
1974	Payment-related benefit	Single woman's allowance Prisoner's wife's allowance	
1977		Supplementary welfare allowance	
1980			National fuel scheme
1984		Family income supplement	
1989		Lone parent's allowance	
1990		Carer's allowance	

leave 4 more rows please

said that schemes were introduced at different times to meet different needs.

The widow's and orphan's pensions (contributory and non-contributory) were introduced in 1935 following a report of the Poor Law Commission in 1927. The social insurance based unemployment benefits scheme (1911) provided benefit only for short-term unemployment, whereas the widespread and prolonged unemployment in the early 1930s inevitably led to the introduction of a means tested assistance scheme to enable the unemployed, who had exhausted their unemployment benefit, to continue to receive a payment (albeit at a reduced rate subject to a means test). The introduction of schemes for women in the early 1970s must be considered against the background of the burgeoning women's movement in Ireland and elsewhere at the time and the recommendations of the *Report of the Commission on the Status of Women* (1972).

With the introduction of the various schemes, the home assistance scheme (derived from the Poor Law) became more and more marginal. Its highly discretionary nature was due to the fact that it was administered by local authorities without formal guidelines from central level.[2] It was a scheme of last resort and one to cater for emergencies. Home assistance, the last link with the nineteenth-century Poor Law, was finally replaced in 1977 by the supplementary welfare allowance, administered by health boards, subject to the control of the Minister for Social Welfare.

In Figure 2.1 a number of miscellaneous schemes which are neither social assistance nor social insurance, may be noted. Two of these, children's allowance (renamed child benefit in 1986) and free travel, are universal schemes. The former, as already indicated, is a scheme whereby monthly payments are made in respect of each child up to age sixteen (age eighteen if in full-time education). Under the free travel scheme all persons of old age pension qualifying age (sixty-six years) are entitled to use public transport facilities (with some exceptions during peak hours in urban areas) free of charge. The electricity allowance is mainly confined to recipients of the old age pension living alone, and qualification for this allowance automatically gives entitlement to a free TV licence (monochrome only). The cheap fuel scheme was introduced during World War II when fuel was scarce and its application was confined to recipients of certain social welfare payments in urban areas, mainly along the eastern seaboard. The scheme remained in existence following the war and the demand for a similar scheme for the rest of the country was met in 1980 with the introduction of a national fuel scheme. Two separate fuel schemes existed until 1988 when a unified scheme was introduced for the entire country.

Modifications to schemes since their inception have been made, mainly related to eligibility conditions being eased. For example, the old age pension introduced in 1909 was described, with some justification, as 'a pension too low at an age too high after a means test which was too severe'.[3] The present situation is quite different; the qualifying age has been reduced from seventy years to sixty-six years (between 1973 and 1977) and the means test has been eased considerably. Apart from increases in the rates of payment, virtually all schemes have been modified since their inception.

Main features of income maintenance system

Social insurance schemes
As already indicated, eligibility for the social insurance schemes is based on social insurance contributions. Up to 1974 the social insurance contribution was in the form of a 'stamp' at a flat rate irrespective of income. In that year a partial pay-related social insurance system (PRSI) was introduced and in 1979 a more comprehensive system was introduced. Contributions are now based on a percentage of earnings up to a certain ceiling. The standard rate of contribution for employees is 5.5 per cent and the ceiling in 1992/93 is £19,000. In a year of uninterrupted employment a person will have fifty-two contributions paid. The rate of contribution for employers is 12.2 per cent per employee up to an income limit of £20,300.

The qualifying conditions vary from scheme to scheme. In general, however, a contribution record over a relatively long period is required for long-term payments, such as the old age pension. This is usually in the form of an average number of contributions paid or credited (see p. 22) over a period. For example, in order to qualify for the maximum rate of old age pension, an average number of forty-eight weeks' PRSI paid or credited from 1953 or from the time insurable employment commenced to the end of the tax year before reaching pensionable age is required.

Qualification for short-term benefits, such as unemployment and disability (sickness), is based on a contribution record of a shorter duration than for the long-term benefits. For example, unemployment benefit is payable if the claimant has at least thirty-nine weeks' PRSI paid or credited in the governing tax year; forty-eight weeks' PRSI paid or credited are required in the governing tax year in order to obtain benefit at the maximum rate.

Apart from contributions which have been paid, provision is also made for credited contributions which apply in certain circumstances. A person on unemployment benefit, for example, may continue to receive credited contributions which, in effect, are the equivalent of paid contributions. Credits help to maintain a social insurance record over a period of unemployment and are an important means of qualifying for long-term benefits.

There are a number of different social insurance classes which determine the rate of contribution. The standard rate of 5.5 per cent is paid by persons in Class A who account for the majority of contributors. Persons in this class are entitled to the full range of social insurance benefits. There are special social insurance categories for others who are not entitled to the same range of benefits. For example, permanent and pensionable civil servants pay a contribution of 0.9 per cent and in return are entitled to a limited number of benefits. The rationale behind the classification of the population into different social insurance classes is related to work status. In the case of civil servants the rationale for not paying the full contribution would appear to be that, having secure employment and consequently being unlikely to be unemployed and having adequate occupational pensions, they do not have to contribute towards such benefits. The end result is a rather complex system of social insurance classes.

A full description of the contribution conditions attached to the various social insurance schemes and details of the social insurance classes are given in *Guide to Social Welfare Services* and *Social Welfare Rates of Payment*, published by the Department of Social Welfare.

Social assistance schemes

Eligibility for all social assistance schemes is determined on the basis of a means test. The amount of means will determine whether a person is entitled to maximum benefit or reduced benefit, or is ineligible for any benefit. Means are assessed by officers of the Department of Social Welfare.

In the assessment of means a number of items are taken into account. These include cash income less certain allowances, value of investments, benefit and privilege (such as the value of board and lodgings). The latter is taken into account only in relation to unemployment assistance and the single woman's allowance in cases where the claimants are residing with their parents. Benefit and privilege is assessed by taking the net parental income (less tax and PRSI contributions) into account. Against this a number of allowances are made, such as outgoings on rent, the interest element of a mortgage and a parental allowance. The remainder of the net income is then divided among the non-earning members of the household, including the applicant. The resulting figure is taken as the value of board and lodgings to the claimant, subject to a maximum assessment of 17 per cent of net parental income. The means of an unemployed school leaver, for example, who applies for unemployment assistance are based on those of his/her parents despite the fact that the school leaver may not have an independent income.

In the assessment of cash income certain payments are excluded – for example, supplementary welfare allowance payments. A portion of earnings is also disregarded in the calculation of means for certain assistance schemes, such as blind pension and widow's pension. The income derived from a dwelling through letting is also taken into account. In relation to farmers, the value of all saleable produce from the farm is taken into account.

Different methods are used for calculating interest from investments (such as bank deposits, stocks and shares) for various social assistance schemes. The schemes are divided into three categories as follows:

(1) For unemployment assistance, smallholder's assistance and the allowance for single women, the yearly value of investments is taken to be 5 per cent of the first £400 and 10 per cent of the balance.

(2) For old age and blind pensions the first £200 is
     excluded and the yearly value is taken to be 5 per cent
     of the next £375 and 10 per cent of the balance. If the
     weekly value is £1 or more, a further £1 is added.

(3) For widow's pension, deserted wife's allowance, lone
     parent's allowance and prisoner's wife's allowance, the
     first £200 is excluded, plus an additional £100 for each
     dependent child and the yearly value is taken to be 5
     per cent of the balance.

The different weekly values arising from the above are best
illustrated by an example. If it is assumed that all applicants
had £1,000 in savings in a bank deposit account then the
value of this sum for applicants in (1) above would be £1.55
per week, for those in (2) it would be £2.20 per week, and
for those in (3) it would be £0.80 per week (70p per week
for an unmarried mother with one child).

For some schemes, such as unemployment assistance and
smallholder's assistance, maximum benefit can only be
obtained by those with no means at all. For other schemes,
means up to a certain amount per person per week are
allowed before entitlement to maximum benefit is affected.
In the case of the old age, blind and widow's pensions,
deserted wife's, unmarried mother's and prisoner's wife's
allowances, the applicant may have means of up to £6 per
week (£12 per week for married couples applying for old
age or blind pensions) and still qualify for the full pension
or allowance. Claimants of the orphan's pension and the
single woman's allowance can have weekly means up to £2
and qualify for maximum benefits. Means in excess of the
permitted amount will lead to reduced benefits. In general,
the reduction is in bands of £2 for every £2 increase in
means. The maximum cut-off point varies according to the
different schemes (see Table 2.1).

For old age and blind pensions a married couple may
have means of up to twice the personal rate while the
number of children will affect the upper limit in the case of
the widow's pension, deserted wife's, lone parent's and
prisoner's wife's allowances. Thus, in 1992 a widow with
more than two children could have weekly means in excess
of £86 and still qualify for some pension.

A summary of the main elements of the means test is

Table 2.1: Major components of means test for social assistance schemes, July 1992

Assistance Scheme	Minimum means allowed before entitlement to full benefit is reduced (£ per week)	Maximum means allowed before entitlement to benefit is removed (£ per week)	Personal income from earnings disregarded (£ per week)	Income disregarded from earnings for each child dependant (£ per week)	Assessment of investments
Unemployment assistance short term/long term	–	53.00/57.20	–	–	5% of first £400 and 10% of balance
Single woman's allowance	12	57.20	–	–	
Old age pension (personal)	6[a]	57.20[a]	–	2	Exclude first £200, 5% of next £375, 10% of balance
Blind pension (personal)	6[a]	57.20[a]	6[c]	2	
Carer's allowance	–	53.00	–	2	
Widow's pension (personal)	6	57.20[b]	–	6	Exclude first £200, 5% of balance [d,e]
Lone parent's allowance	6	57.20[b]	–	6	
Deserted wife's allowance	6	57.20[b]	–	6	
Prisoner's wife's allowance	6	57.20[b]	–	6	

a   This amount is doubled in the case of a married couple.
b   The number of children affects the maximum means, i.e. the more children the higher the maximum means.
c   An additional £4 is disregarded if the blind person is married.
d   If the weekly value of investments is £1 or more another £1 is added.
e   A further £100 is excluded in respect of each dependent child.

contained in Table 2.1. The details of the means require-
ments for particular schemes are given in the *Guide to Social
Welfare Services* published by the Department of Social
Welfare.

While a number of modifications to the means test took
place in the early 1970s there have been few amendments
since then. By any standard the system of means test could
only be described as complex. It is extremely doubtful if it
is fully understood by many claimants.

Other social welfare schemes
Apart from the social insurance and social assistance
schemes, reference has already been made to a number of
miscellaneous schemes administered by the Department of
Social Welfare. The most notable of these is the system of
child benefit (formerly known as children's allowance).

Children's allowance was introduced in 1944 and the
monthly allowance was paid in respect of the third and subsequent children. In introducing the Bill in the Dáil, the
Minister for Industry and Commerce, Mr Seán Lemass,
gave the following as the rationale for the scheme:

> The basis of the argument in favour of the establishment of
> a children's allowance scheme is that among the causes of
> want, apart from unemployment, ill-health (etc.), there is
> the fact that in an economic system such as ours, where
> wages are related to standards of productivity or determined
> by supply and demand, the amount the wage earner can
> obtain is frequently inadequate to provide for the reason-
> able requirements of a large family ... it is, I think, necessary
> to emphasise that the basis of the whole case for the
> establishment of a children's allowance service is the need
> of large families.[4]

Subsequently, various changes have been made to the
scheme and it has frequently been the subject of criticism
on the grounds that it should be applied more selectively.
There has been strong opposition to treating child benefit
as taxable income, introducing some form of means test, or
a qualifying income ceiling. For some time a system of child
tax allowance existed alongside children's allowance. In
1984 the government pledged to introduce a unified system
of child benefit.[5] This unified system, however, was not

introduced but the tax allowance, whose value had been reduced over a period of time, was eventually abolished in 1986 and children's allowance was renamed child benefit. One of the important differences between child benefit and other social welfare payments is that increases in the rates of payment of child benefit are treated quite separately. In other words, increases in general social welfare payments are not necessarily applied in the case of child benefit.

Beneficiaries of social welfare
An important feature of the Irish income maintenance system is that once a claimant has established entitlement, payments are also generally made in respect of any adult and child dependants. This has been a traditional feature of the system and was only modified following the implementation of an EC directive in 1986 on the equal treatment of men and women. Up to then spouses (mostly married women) were regarded as being financially dependent. With the greater participation by married women in the labour force, however, the situation had changed over a period of time but this change was not reflected in the income maintenance system. Thus, if a man became unemployed and qualified for unemployment benefit he received a personal rate together with an adult dependant rate even if his wife was employed and earning a relatively high income. In compliance with the directive, the situation was changed amid considerable controversy at the end of 1986.

An adult dependant is now defined as someone who is either not earning or is earning less than £55 per week. The situation with regard to payment for child dependants has also altered. In short, if a full personal rate and adult dependant allowance is payable, then the full child dependant allowance is payable. If, however, the spouse is not regarded as an adult dependant (as defined above), then only half the child dependant allowance is payable for each child.

The above brief description of the situation in relation to dependants in the income maintenance system is a necessary prelude to understanding trends in the number of beneficiaries. Recipients, together with their adult and child dependants, constitute the beneficiaries.

Over the past twenty-five years the number of beneficiaries has more than doubled (Table 2.2). Recipients of
child benefit are not included in these figures. In 1966 the
566,000 beneficiaries accounted for 20 per cent of the total
population and by 1991 this had increased to 1.39 million
or 39 per cent of the population.

This does not imply, of course, that over one-third of the
population is solely dependent on social welfare payments.
Some of those in receipt of social insurance payments, such
as old age pensioners, may well have another source of
income and in practice it is only those on the maximum
rates of social assistance payments who rely almost exclusively on social welfare payments for their livelihood.

In general terms, the growth in the number of beneficiaries is accounted for by a number of factors. Of these,
the increase in unemployment is by far the most significant,
accounting for half of the growth between 1966 and 1991.
Other factors include the introduction of new schemes and
the modification of eligibility conditions. The largest proportionate increases were among unmarried mothers and
deserted wives.

The growth in unemployment is reflected in the composition of the social welfare population. In 1966 the unemployed and their dependants accounted for one-quarter of
the total, whereas in 1991 this had increased to two-fifths.
Recipients of old age and retirement pensions now account
for one-fifth of the total as compared with one-third in 1966.

Financing and expenditure
As already indicated, a distinction can be made between the
financing of the social insurance schemes and the financing of the social assistance schemes.

Social insurance schemes are financed from pay-related
social insurance contributions from employers and
employees with the state making good any deficit on outgoings from general taxation. Financing of social assistance
schemes is from general taxation. Employer and employee
PRSI contributions go into the social insurance fund (see
Table 2.3). The tripartite system of funding of social
insurance (employers/employees/state) is not based on
any set formula. In practice, the shares have fluctuated over
time. The White Paper, *Social Security* (1949), argued that

Table 2.2: Number of beneficiaries[a] of weekly social welfare payments, 1966-1991

	1966	1982	1991
Old age pension (contributory)	57,343	93,889	93,004
Retirement pension	–	47,041	72,880
Old age pension (non-contributory)	124,342	143,333	127,434
Pre-retirement allowance	–	–	16,477
Disability benefit	123,013	132,972	112,913
Invalidity pension	–	42,215	69,107
Injury benefit	–	2,179	2,365
Interim disability benefit	–	–	2,863
Disablement benefit	–	5,351	8,161
Death benefit	–	419	789
Widow's pension (contributory)	55,359	94,205	97,968
Widow's pension (non-contributory)	29,554	19,679	18,356
Deserted wife's benefit	–	9,687	31,624
Deserted wife's allowance	–	8,030	1,895[b]
Unmarried mother's allowance	–	16,843	–[b]
Prisoner's wife's allowance	–	622	12[b]
Lone parent's allowance	–	–	75,735[b]
Maternity benefit	1,046	1,331	5,421
Orphan's allowance (contributory)	461	913	697
Orphan's allowance (non-contributory)	156	140	143
Supplementary welfare allowance	29,818	40,929	30,593
Family income supplement	–	–	32,973
Carer's allowance	–	–	5,520
Unemployment benefit	85,608	187,814	159,259
Unemployment assistance	59,742[c]	189,152	379,440
Smallholder's assistance	–	71,191	41,436
Single woman's allowance	–	2,982	1,981
Rent allowance	–	–	1,004
Total	566,442	1,110,917	1,390,050

a Recipients, adult dependants and child dependants
b In 1990 the lone parent's allowance was introduced and this led to the amalgamation of certain schemes. All recipients of unmarried mother's allowance and deserted husband's allowance and widower's non-contributory pension transferred to the scheme. Recipients with children on widow's non-contributory pension, deserted wife's allowance and prisoner's wife's allowance also transferred to the lone parent's allowance.
c Includes approximately 7,000 on smallholder's assistance.

the fund should be financed equally by employers,
employees and the state.[6] This recommendation was not
acted upon. In 1975 the Minister for Finance, Richie Ryan,
stated:

> The government have decided in principle to transfer the
> exchequer contribution towards the cost of social insurance
> to the other contributors to the social insurance fund over a
> period of six years or so.[7]

This was not acted upon either. The employer share is now
considerably higher than two decades ago (see Table 2.3).

When the financing of the social assistance schemes is
allied to that of the social insurance schemes, the state's
contribution to the total system is relatively high (Table 2.4).

Administration

Prior to the National Insurance Act, 1911, a number of
societies provided schemes for sickness benefit. Following
the Act, sickness and unemployment benefit schemes continued to be operated mainly by these existing societies
under the general supervision of the Irish Insurance
Commissioners. A statutory condition of admittance to the
scheme was that a society be non-profit-making. Commercial
insurance companies which formed separate non-profit-
making branches also became engaged in the scheme. By
1933 the number of insured persons in the state was about
474,000 and these were catered for by sixty-five approved
societies with membership ranging from fifty-five in a small
mutual benefit society up to over 100,000 in a central society
covering the whole country.[8] Societies had considerable
freedom in selecting workers to be admitted to membership
and some societies were relatively more prosperous than
others. The latter, by accumulating reserves, were able to
increase the statutory cash benefits while at the other end of
the scale some small societies had difficulty even in meeting
the statutory benefits.

Apart from these differences between societies, the
administrative costs of the scheme were also relatively high.
The National Health Insurance Act, 1933, made provision
for the amalgamation of all societies into a single society –
the National Health Insurance Society. In 1947 the Depart-

Table 2.3: Sources of income for social insurance fund, 1967-1991* (%)

	1967/68 (£34.8m)	1980 (£501m)	1985 (£1,229.2m)	1991 (£1,516.2m)
Employer	30.5	53.2	48.0	60.1
Employee	29.1	22.1	23.0	26.2
Self-employed	–	–	–	3.9
State	38.1	24.5	28.8	9.6
Other receipts	2.3	0.2	0.2	0.2
Total	100.0	100.0	100.0	100.0

* Up to 1990 the occupational injuries insurance was not included in the above figures. It was funded solely by employers from a separate fund. In 1990 this fund was amalgamated with the social insurance fund and this accounts for the increase in the employers' share and the drop in the state's share.

Source: Reports of the Department of Social Welfare

Table 2.4: Sources of income for all expenditure on social welfare, 1967-1991* (%)

	1967/68 (£67.6m)	1980 (£872.6m)	1985 (£2,247.3m)	1991 (£3,092.5m)
Employer	18.4	31.8	26.2	29.5
Employee	14.5	12.4	12.6	12.8
Self-employed	–	–	–	1.9
State	65.3	55.4	61.0	55.7
Other receipts	1.8	0.4	0.2	0.1
Total	100.0	100.0	100.0	100.0

* The occupational injuries insurance was not included in these figures until 1990.

Source: Reports of the Department of Social Welfare

ment of Social Welfare was established and all social insurance and assistance functions previously performed by the Departments of Local Government and Public Health (e.g. old age pensions, widow's and orphan's pensions) and Industry and Commerce (e.g. unemployment assistance, children's allowance) were transferred to the new Department. The National Health Insurance Society was dissolved in 1950 and its functions taken over by the Minister for Social Welfare. The Social Welfare Act, 1952, established a unified social insurance scheme, replacing the separate schemes for unemployment, national health and widow's and orphan's pensions. The net effect of these changes was not only to simplify administrative procedures and reduce costs but also to ensure that one government minister would be responsible for the overall direction of all social insurance and assistance schemes.

While the Department of Social Welfare has overall responsibility, the cooperation of other government agencies is essential to the administration of the income maintenance system. An Post, through its extensive network of post offices, provides outlets for payments such as child benefit and old age pensions. The Department of Justice, through the Garda Síochána, also assists by certifying evidence of unemployment for claimants who live more than six miles from a social welfare office. The Revenue Commissioners collect the pay-related social insurance contributions from employers and employees.

Links with some agencies, however, appear to have long outlived their usefulness or relevance. The Old Age Pension Act of 1908 provided for the establishment of pension committees in each borough and urban district with a population of 10,000 or over and in each county. Members of pension committees were appointed by the local authority and often included elected representatives of the authority. The committee's function was to consider and determine, subject to a right of appeal, all claims to a pension and all questions as to continued entitlement to a pension. Since no similar procedure applied to other schemes, the continued existence of these committees served to highlight their anachronistic features. They were eventually abolished in 1985. Similarly, despite the transfer of the day-to-day administration of the supplementary welfare allowance scheme from local authorities to health boards, subject to the general control of the Department of Social Welfare, the local authorities were still expected to contribute towards the cost of a scheme they no longer administered! Furthermore, by the time this practice was abolished in 1986, local authorities were deriving the bulk of their income from the same source as the Department of Social Welfare, i.e. the exchequer. The fact that health boards are administering the supplementary welfare allowance scheme still gives rise to certain difficulties (see p. 39).

Appeals system
The appeals system is an important element of the administration of the income maintenance system. This is designed to safeguard the rights of claimants who feel they have been unfairly refused payment or awarded less than the maximum payment. Appeals are dealt with by appeals officers and may be decided summarily (especially those dealing with contribution records) or orally.

In 1990 a total of 15,871 appeals were received, of which almost half (49 per cent) related to eligibility for unemployment assistance. The number of annual appeals constitutes a relatively small proportion of the total number of annual claims (Table 2.5). The 15,871 appeals in 1990 accounted for 1.5 per cent of total claims (1,080,873). It has not been the practice of the Department of Social Welfare to publish statistics on the outcome of appeals but it has been established that, across the various schemes, between one-third and one-half of appeals result in a favourable decision for the claimant.[9] In 1990 a separate Appeals Office was established (see p. 42).

Commission on Social Welfare
Given the central role of the income maintenance schemes

Table 2.5: Number of claims* and appeals received by the Department of Social Welfare, 1984-1990

	Claims	Appeals
1984	1,149,601	19,349
1985	1,174,050	17,288
1986	1,180,490	18,095
1987	1,222,860	20,371
1988	1,158,498	19,747
1989	1,078,534	18,548
1990	1,080,873	15,871

* Excluding claims for 'free schemes', such as free travel, electricity allowance and free phone rental.

Source: Reports of the Department of Social Welfare

in the lives of so many, the considerable public expenditure involved and the piecemeal development of the system, it is surprising that no fundamental review had taken place before the establishment of the Commission on Social Welfare in 1983. This is in marked contrast to other areas such as health and education. Admittedly, three official reports on the system were published, a White Paper, *Social Security* (1949), and two Green Papers, *A National Income-Related Pension Scheme* (1976) and *Social Insurance for the Self-Employed* (1978). In addition, a special committee was established to examine the system of workmen's compensation arising from occupational injuries and its report was published in 1962. Otherwise, the system was not subject to the periodic review which has been characteristic of other areas. Nor was there any popular demand for reform. The main areas of concern to particular groups were the rates of payment and these would be the subject of pre-budget submissions. In 1982 the National Social Services Board in its pre-budget submission called for the establishment of a commission to carry out a fundamental review of the system.[10] A commitment to establish such a commission was part of the programme of the Fine Gael/Labour coalition government which came into office in December 1982. The main term of reference of the Commission on Social Welfare, established in 1983 under the chairmanship of John Curry, was:

> To review and report on the social welfare system and related social services and to make recommendations for their development having regard to the needs of modern Irish society.

The Commission, whose report was published in 1986, opted for an evolutionary rather than a radical change to the system. It envisaged reforms within the framework of the existing system rather than replacing the system. At no stage had any guiding principles been laid down for the income maintenance system. The Commission therefore considered that the principles which should guide the development of the system were adequacy, redistribution, comprehensiveness, consistency, and simplicity. Under the principle of adequacy, the payment levels should be adequate in relation to prevailing living standards.

Redistribution is effected, not only through the system of payments, but also through general taxation and social insurance contributions which finance the payments. Comprehensiveness implies that significant categories of need should not be excluded from the payment structure; the sense of entitlement to payment, once the qualifying conditions have been met, is also an essential element of comprehensiveness. Consistency implies that, as far as possible, policies in other areas should be broadly consistent with those of the income maintenance system and that there should of course be internal consistency in the system. Finally, simplicity implies that the system should be easily understood by both claimants and administrators. The reformed system, as proposed by the Commission, reflects a mix of these principles but with an emphasis on the principle of adequacy.

Key elements of proposed reform
The four key elements of the reformed system proposed by the Commission concerned the payment structure, social insurance, social assistance and financing.

The payment structure
The most fundamental issue which faced the Commission was the adequacy of payments. There had never been any official attempt to establish what a minimally adequate income should be for a person dependent on income maintenance. The payment structure has simply evolved without any explicit reference to particular indicators such as wage levels. Since the early 1970s, however, there has been a conscious attempt to ensure that increases in payments are in line with inflation.

By using a number of indicators the Commission estimated that a minimally adequate income for a single person in 1985 was in the range of £50 to £60 per week (the top point being equivalent to approximately half the net average industrial earnings). The Commission recognised that its calculation of a minimally adequate income could be open to criticism but stated:

> ... in the absence of any explicit official criteria and because of the limitations of available data we had no option but to

attempt to establish a minimally adequate income. Not to have done so would, in our view, have been a serious omission. Furthermore, if our approach is considered to be deficient then an acceptable alternative should be provided.[11]

Some of the existing payments were well below the estimated minimally adequate income while others were at or near the top part of the range. The Commission was faced with a variety of payment levels for different categories and contingencies for which there was no apparent rationale. The lowest payment (unemployment assistance) in the system for a single person was 60 per cent of the highest payment (old age contributory pension). Inevitably, incongruous situations arose where, for example, a person long-term unemployed with a dependent spouse and two children received considerably less than a couple on old age pensions.

The variation in rates of payment for different categories mainly arises from piecemeal changes over time rather than any systematic evaluation of the income needs of particular categories. The result was a payment structure which was not only complex but also discriminated against individuals and families with similar financial needs. A hierarchical system existed with the highest payments going to the elderly, followed by widows and with the unemployed at the bottom. Insofar as there was any rationale for the different rates of payment it may have had more to do with popular notions of need in Irish society and of attitudes towards groups which were regarded as 'deserving' and 'undeserving' poor. The Commission recommended that, in general, the same basic payment should apply to all recipients with the main difference being a differential of the order of 10 per cent between insurance and assistance payments.

A number of other issues arose in the context of the payment structure. The Commission made recommendations on each of these designed to bring a greater degree of consistency into the system. Thus, for example, there were no less than thirty-six different rates of child dependant payments depending on the birth order of the child and the recipient category of the parent. The lowest child dependant payment was 42 per cent of the highest and children of widows attracted the highest amounts. In the

Commission's view, the range was unjustified and it recommended a rationalisation of child dependant payments. Similarly, the Commission argued that the existing limited pay-related element (associated with some payments only) should be phased out and the priority should be the attainment of a minimally adequate income for all recipients.

Social insurance
The Commission favoured the retention of the social insurance system. The *raison d'être* of social insurance has never been sufficiently articulated in Ireland. For this reason the Commission emphasised that social insurance was an expression of social solidarity and citizenship in which the risks, costs and benefits are spread as widely as possible in the community. Furthermore, in the Commission's view, social insurance contributions create a sense of entitlement to benefit and generate support among the community for these benefits. The Commission recommended that all income earners should therefore contribute to and benefit where appropriate from social insurance. The main group outside the social insurance system when the report was published was the self-employed, including farmers, who accounted for about 20 per cent of the labour force.

Apart from the self-employed, there were other smaller groups not liable for social insurance contributions, such as members of religious orders and certain ministers of religion. Furthermore, public servants are liable only for a modified rate of contribution on grounds that their conditions of employment do not warrant coverage for all benefits. The Commission recommended that public servants be liable for the full rate of contribution.

Social assistance
The widening of coverage for social insurance as proposed by the Commission would lead to a decline in the need for means tested social assistance payments. Social assistance would then be a residual element in the income maintenance system.

The Commission recommended that there should be a comprehensive social assistance scheme for those who, for whatever reason, do not qualify for social insurance. The main condition would be the establishment of an income need irrespective of the cause of that need. This would lead to the elimination of the unnecessary categorical social assistance schemes which exist at present (e.g. lone parent's allowance, widow's pension, prisoner's wife's allowance). The income need would, as now, be established by reference to a means test. As already noted, the existing means test is complex and is applied differentially to the various categories of claimants. The Commission recommended that the means test be rationalised, simplified and that the main constituents be better publicised.

Financing
It has already been noted that the social insurance system in Ireland is funded on a tripartite basis by employers, employees and the state and that social assistance is funded entirely by the state out of general taxation. There is no set formula which determines the apportionment of costs between the three partners to the social insurance fund nor did the Commission support the notion of pre-stated shares.

While the Commission recognised that social insurance is not directly comparable with private commercial insurance, it nevertheless has a significant insurance dimension which is not outweighed by the absence of an actuarial link between benefits and contributions. The Commission also considered the question of the employment effects of employers' social insurance contributions, a subject of debate on a number of occasions in recent years. In the Commission's view, the evidence concerning the effects on employment was inconclusive. Nor did it justify a departure from the payroll base of contributions which the Commission concluded was the broadest, most clearly identifiable and most predictable base available.

On grounds of redistribution the Commission concluded that the income ceiling on contributions should be gradually abolished. This move would need to be co-ordinated with the evolution of earnings and income tax.

Other issues
The Commission also considered a series of issues related to the key elements of the proposed reform. These included issues affecting particular groups such as the

unemployed, the elderly and lone parents. In relation to the unemployed, for example, the Commission did not consider the existing administrative procedures governing conditions of entitlement to unemployment payments to be appropriate given the high level of unemployment. This applies especially to those which require the unemployed to attend at an employment exchange at least once weekly in order to 'sign on', indicate their availability for employment, and collect their payment. The Commission recommended a more flexible approach and the need to provide all recipients with the greatest possible choice in relation to method of payment.

A considerable degree of duplication of functions exists between the Department of Social Welfare and the Department of Health. While the Department of Social Welfare is mainly concerned with providing a range of cash benefits, it is also responsible for 'treatment benefits' (dental, ophthalmic and aural), based on social insurance contributions. These are more properly health functions. Similarly, the Department of Health, through the eight regional health boards, administers a number of cash payments. This in turn gives rise to a lack of consistency and uniformity in the application of guidelines since, in effect, the health boards are autonomous agencies. Particular problems arise in the case of the supplementary welfare allowance scheme (formerly home assistance), administered by health boards, where discretion is an important element. The Commission recommended that all income maintenance functions be transferred to the Department of Social Welfare, and the 'treatment benefits' transferred to the Department of Health. Ironically, when the views of the two Departments on this matter were sought by the Commission it emerged that the principle of the transfer of functions had been agreed for some time but that no concrete steps had been taken to effect the transfer.

Because of the nature of the service the Commission's view was that the income maintenance system should be organised to respond in an efficient manner to the client population. A survey based on the experiences and perceptions of claimants was commissioned and this highlighted a number of deficiencies, especially the delay in processing claims. The Commission considered that computerisation was a key factor in the development of a more efficient and more localised service and envisaged a situation where the entire application process could be conducted locally. Delays were encountered because of the transfer of claimant files to and from central offices in Dublin. The efficient delivery of the service must be balanced by a need for control measures and a number of recommendations were made to limit the scope for fraud.

The appeals function is an important aspect of the income maintenance system. In the Commission's view there was a perception that the appeals system was not independent since it operated within the Department of Social Welfare. Furthermore, statistics on appeals were published as part of the Department's biennial report but consisted simply of numbers of appeals heard under different categories with no information on the outcome of appeals. The Commission recommended the establishment of an Appeals Office as a separate executive office with a requirement that it publish an annual report containing not only adequate statistics on appeals but, where necessary, policy recommendations.

Priority recommendations

While the Commission had estimated that additional revenue could be generated from broadening the social insurance base, there would be a net cost to the exchequer from implementing its recommendations. Partly, though not exclusively for cost reasons, the Commission recommended that the development of the reformed system be undertaken on a gradual basis.

In this context four areas were considered to merit priority attention. These were as follows:

- improvement in the basic payment for those on the lowest payments to narrow the unacceptable differences which existed in payment levels between different categories of recipients
- the provision of more adequate support for families especially those long-term dependent on social welfare
- the broadening of the social insurance base
- the accelerated development of computerisation and the upgrading of premises in which income maintenance services are delivered.

Prospects for reform

The government statement issued on publication of the Commission's report in August 1986 noted that:

> ... in present circumstances and for the immediate future it would be beyond the capacity of the country to fully implement the Commission's proposals. This is an unpalatable reality but it must be borne in mind in the context of considering all the Commission's proposals.

This statement gave the impression that the Commission's report was going to be ignored by government. Subsequently, the Minister for Social Welfare, Gemma Hussey, stated in the Dáil that:

> ... there is no question of the report being dismissed or ignored. There is absolutely no doubt that radical changes will be necessary over the next few years in the social welfare system ... While we must be selective in bringing forward proposals for additional expenditure, there is considerable scope for reform of the system in line with the general approach which the Commission has adopted.[12]

While the government's initial reaction to the report appeared to be hostile there was a general welcome for the thrust of its recommendations from a variety of organisations. The apparent rejection of the report by the government led to the formation of a coalition of over twenty voluntary groups – Campaign for Welfare Reform – to lobby for the implementation of its recommendations. The notion of the minimally adequate income was highlighted in the debate which ensued and the figure proposed by the Commission was not challenged.

Following the change of government in 1987 some progress began to be made on the recommendations. Thus, the budgets of 1989 to 1992 provided for higher increases for those on the lowest rates of payment. This had the effect of significantly narrowing the gap between the highest and lowest payment (see Table 2.6). The number of different rates of payment for dependent children was rationalised considerably – from thirty-six rates in 1988 to three rates in 1991. In 1988, the self-employed, members of religious orders and all ministers of religion became liable

Table 2.6: Trends in highest and lowest payments in the social welfare system, 1985-1992

Maximum personal rate of payment (weekly)	1985 £	1988 £	1990 £	1992 £	% increase 1985-1992
A. Highest payment (contributory old age pensions over 80 years)	54.90	60.60	65.60	71.00	29.3
B. Lowest payment (unemployment assistance short duration*)	32.75	39.00	45.00	53.00	61.8
B as % of A	59.6%	64.4%	68.7%	74.6%	

*Up to 1989 there was a distinction in the personal and married rates for unemployment assistance between urban and rural areas. In 1985 the rural personal rate was £31.75. The distinction was abolished in 1989 and the rural rate increased to the same level as the urban.

for social insurance contributions. This was perhaps the most significant development in the income maintenance system; it had seemed, for some time, as if the political will to bring these groups into the system was lacking. Other developments were the introduction of a lone parent social assistance scheme in 1989 and a carer's allowance in 1990. The lone parent scheme represented a move towards a more rational system of income support for lone parents, including male lone parents with dependent children.

The Social Welfare Act of 1990 provided for the establishment of a separate Appeals Office, headed by a director and chief appeals officer, as an executive office of the Department of Social Welfare. The establishment of the Appeals Office was designed to emphasise the independence of the appeals system and to ensure that it was perceived to be impartial and independent. In accordance with the Commission's recommendations, the Appeals Office is obliged to publish an annual report on its activities with comment, where necessary, on the workings of the social welfare system and the implications of its decisions for policy making.

Various groups have continued to use the *Report of the Commission on Social Welfare* in their pre-budget submissions and as a yardstick to evaluate reforms in the system. Of greatest significance perhaps was the commitment made in the *Programme for Economic and Social Progress,* agreed between the government and the social partners (trade unions, employers' organisations and farmers' organisations) in 1991, to implement the priority recommendations of the Commission's report over a three-year period.[13] While progress had been made in relation to certain recommendations of the Commission up to then, this was the first commitment at official level to implement the Commission's priority recommendations.

It can be argued that, following decades of piecemeal development, the *Report of the Commission on Social Welfare* provided a blueprint for the rational development of the income maintenance system.

Income poverty
Income is not the sole determining factor of poverty but it is nonetheless an important constituent, irrespective of how poverty is defined. While there is no universally accepted definition of poverty it is most popularly regarded as lack of sufficient income. But what might be regarded as poverty in developed countries could be quite different to that in, for example, an underdeveloped Third World country.

It is now accepted in various research reports that poverty is viewed as exclusion, through lack of resources, from the generally approved standards and styles of living in society as a whole. This approach is based on the fact that perceptions of acceptable and minimum standards change over time and between countries with varying levels of per capita incomes. Townsend, one of the foremost writers on the subject, has defined poverty in relative terms, the poor being:

> Individuals and families whose resources, over time, fall seriously short of the resources commanded by the average individual or family in the community in which they live.[14]

Measurement of poverty
If poverty is defined in relative terms it follows that the

measurement of the extent of poverty is usually formulated in relation to average incomes in society. Thus, for example, some countries estimate the extent of poverty as the proportion of households/families whose income falls below half of mean income in the population in general. Use of half average income, however, is no more than convention – it has no analytical basis. Furthermore, the use of a poverty threshold (such as 50 per cent or 60 per cent of mean income) does not give an authoritative 'poverty line', i.e. a line below which people are poor. In practice the term 'poverty line' is used popularly but has no official or precise meaning.

Various studies have been carried out in Ireland since the early 1970s to estimate the proportion of the population living in poverty. The most recent study is based on a survey in 1987 among households and was undertaken by the Economic and Social Research Institute for the Combat Poverty Agency.[15] The study used different cut-off points to measure the extent of poverty. On this basis the Combat Poverty Agency concluded that one-third of the population was living in poverty (i.e. below 60 per cent of mean income). It also emerged that households headed by the unemployed, families with several children and farming households were the three main groupings vulnerable to poverty. This study also noted by reference to previous research that from 1973 to 1978 the percentage of households below the 50 per cent poverty line fell marginally, while the percentage increased from 1980 to 1987. A further key finding was that the risk of poverty for families with four or more children had more than doubled over the period 1973 to 1987 and this was largely attributed to the rise in unemployment. By contrast the risk of poverty among the elderly had declined, and this was associated with real improvement in state pensions.

In the context of the high risk of poverty among families with children, the NESC argued for an integrated approach to family income support in place of the variety of existing measures, e.g. child benefit, child dependant allowances and family income supplement. As a first step the NESC recommended greater targeting among low income families. This would be achieved by increasing the level of the monthly child benefit (paid to all families) which would then be taxable. The effect would be to ensure that low income families were the beneficiaries of the increase while at the same time achieving a system of income support which was more neutral as between employment and unemployment.[16]

Poverty as an issue
In the 1950s and 1960s several studies appeared in the USA which indicated that, despite increasing affluence following World War II, poverty and inequalities still persisted. This 'rediscovery', as Sinfield[17] described it, led to poverty becoming a socially accepted subject for debate and research, to the establishment of pressure groups and eventually to attempts by governments to find a solution to the problem. In Ireland, poverty may be said to have been 'rediscovered' at a conference on poverty organised by the Council for Social Welfare and held in Kilkenny in 1971. The conference sparked off what was to be a growing national debate on how the plight of the poor in society could be resolved. Perhaps the most important paper read at the conference was 'The Extent of Poverty in Ireland' by Seamus Ó Cinnéide, in which the author estimated that at least one-quarter of the population was living below the poverty line, which was based on income maintenance rates of payment in Ireland (the Republic and Northern Ireland in 1971).[18] The social, cultural and educational deprivation associated with poverty was described in other conference papers.[19] It was felt that the causes and effects of poverty in Ireland were not clearly understood and that there was need for further research.

Thereafter the issue became politicised and was taken up, especially by the Labour Party, which with Fine Gael formed the coalition government of 1973-77.[20] In the pre-election joint policy statement of the two parties, one of the fourteen points referred to the elimination of poverty and the ending of social injustice as major priorities. At the government's instigation, the Social Action Programme of the EC was expanded to include pilot anti-poverty schemes. In 1974, Frank Cluskey, Parliamentary Secretary to the Minister for Social Welfare and a member of the Labour Party, established an advisory committee, the National Committee on Pilot Schemes to Combat Poverty (NCPSCP), to initiate and coordinate pilot schemes to combat poverty.

The Committee became known popularly as Combat Poverty and within a short time became, in effect, an executive body which planned and administered projects and employed the necessary staff. The objectives of Combat Poverty were:

• to bring about practical intervention in areas of deprivation or among groups in need
• to increase public awareness of the problems of poverty
• to contribute to the evolution of effective, long-term policies against poverty.

Of the various projects initiated by Combat Poverty, Ó Cinnéide concluded that: 'One is left with an impression of real but unspecifiable gains for a few'.[21] He also pointed out that the greatest failure of Combat Poverty was that it did not increase public awareness of poverty.

At the end of 1980 the work of Combat Poverty was terminated partly because EC funds for further projects were no longer available. In the Committee's final report it called for the establishment of a national agency to further develop and expand the work of the pilot schemes.

In 1986 the Combat Poverty Agency was established on a statutory basis, reporting to the Minister for Social Welfare. Under the Act, the Agency has four general functions:

• advice and recommendations to the Minister (for Social Welfare) on all aspects of economic and social planning in relation to poverty
• initiation and evaluation of measures aimed at overcoming poverty
• promotion, commission and interpretation of research into poverty
• promotion of greater public understanding of poverty.

The Agency recognised that, because of limits on the resources available, it could not be a major funding source for measures designed to tackle the problem of poverty. Instead it viewed its role as clarifying the causes and effects of poverty and pointing towards solutions.[22]

Since its establishment, the Agency has commissioned various studies on aspects of poverty and has been to the forefront in highlighting poverty issues. It has, for example, on several occasions focused attention on the importance of the adequacy of social welfare payments.

3

Housing

Introduction

One of the central features of the Irish housing system is the predominance of owner occupation or privately owned dwellings. This is due in part to the promotion of owner occupation by successive governments through various measures. There has been state intervention in housing since the middle of the last century and in fact such intervention is now very extensive.

At a general level it can be said that government intervention in the housing area is necessary to ensure that certain standards are maintained, that environmental interests are protected, and that persons without sufficient income are provided with housing.

In housing there is an official statement of the fundamental objectives of policy:

> The government are committed to pursuing housing policies with the broad objective of ensuring that every household has a dwelling suitable to its needs, located in an acceptable environment, at a price or rent it can afford.[1]

Administration

The Department of the Environment (formerly the Department of Local Government, established in 1924) is the central authority responsible for national housing policy. It exercises a general supervision over the social, financial and technical aspects of local authority and private housing and is responsible for the distribution of most of the capital and subsidies for housing provided by the state. The Department also promotes legislation on housing, coordinates the activities of local authorities and is responsible for legislation on building standards.

There are eighty-seven local authorities engaged in the provision of public housing – four county borough councils, twenty-seven county councils² and fifty-six urban district councils. A number of other government departments are concerned with housing, though this is only a minor element of their work. These include, for example, Roinn na Gaeltachta, which pays grants for the building and improvement of dwellings in the Gaeltacht areas.

Major trends in housing output
In this section the major trends in housing development are outlined.³

Housing prior to 1921

Urban housing
The first series of legislative enactments dealing with housing was passed in the 1850s and 1860s. While these and other Acts passed in the 1870s provided a strong legislative basis for a housing drive, little was accomplished under these Acts except in Dublin city. The Housing of the Working Classes Act, 1890, was a more comprehensive measure which repealed practically all the preceding Acts and made a serious effort to deal with the problems of urban housing and slum clearance. The next important piece of legislation dealing with urban housing was the Housing of the Working Classes (Ireland) Act, 1908. This Act set up the first subsidy system for urban housing. The Irish Housing Fund was established, a sum of £180,000 invested, and the income directed towards the cost of dwellings erected after the 1908 Act. By 1919 only 8,700 houses had been provided under the 1908 Act.

In 1921 the problem of urban housing still remained unsolved. A survey of housing needs in municipal areas carried out in 1919 estimated that 46,416 houses were required, one-third of them to replace inhabited houses unfit and incapable of being made fit for human habitation.

Rural housing
The first attempts to improve rural housing in Ireland were

aimed at getting landlords to take the initiative in building cottages for their own tenants. The Dwellings for Labouring Classes (Ireland) Act, 1860, enabled landlords to obtain loans for the provision of cottages.

The census of 1881 indicated that there were 215,000 cottiers and the majority of dwellings in which they lived were single-room cabins with mud walls and thatched roofs. Under the Labourers (Ireland) Act, 1883, housing operations were to be carried out locally by the rural sanitary authorities, the boards of guardians, under the general supervision of the Local Government Board for Ireland. The provision of cottages was no longer left to the initiative of individual landlords or farmers. By 1921 approximately 48,000 cottages had been erected.

Private housing
The demand for private dwellings was stimulated by the Small Dwellings Acquisition Act, 1899, which enabled local authorities to advance loans for the purchase of existing houses. Building societies became another source of finance for house purchase and the main Act governing these societies was passed in 1874. Banks and insurance companies also provided finance in this period. The total number of owner occupiers at the time, however, was small and most of the houses were purchased by investors and let to tenants. A significant development was the introduction, under the Housing Act, 1919, of a scheme of grants for persons who constructed houses in accordance with prescribed conditions. The political conditions of the time prevented the extensive use of the scheme. Nevertheless, the scheme marks one of the first steps in direct state aid to the house purchaser, a policy which has since been sustained and which accounts in part for the relatively high proportion of owner occupied dwellings in Ireland at present.

Housing in the 1920s
The first real attempt to provide houses on a large scale was made by the Free State government which initiated what is referred to as the 'Million Pound Scheme'. Under this scheme local authorities were required to provide £125,000 from rates (local taxation) and raise a further sum of

£375,000 by way of short-term loans from banks, giving a total of £½ million. This was matched by £1 million in state aid and enabled 2,000 houses to be built at an average total cost of £750 per house.

Under the Housing Act, 1924, grants were again made available to people constructing their own dwellings. This Act also empowered local authorities to supplement the state grants by further grants or loans and also free or cheap sites for development work and provided for the partial remission of rates over nineteen years on grant-aided houses. Reconstruction grants were also made available under the 1924 Act.

The housing problem of urban areas, however, remained to be tackled in earnest. A survey carried out by urban authorities in 1929 indicated that almost 44,000 houses were required and highlighted the need for slum clearance.

Housing in the 1930s
The main drive against slums was begun in the 1930s. The Housing Acts, 1931 and 1932, were particularly important, giving effect to the recommendations of previous commissions of enquiry on slum clearance and compulsory acquisition of land and providing greater financial assistance to local authorities for rehousing displaced families.

The output of housing rose steadily during the 1930s reaching a peak of 17,000 in the year ended 31 March 1939. Between 1931 and 1942 a total of 82,000 dwellings were built. During the same period over 11,000 condemned houses were demolished by local authorities as well as an unknown number by others. This period was one of the most productive ever in the building of corporation houses in Dublin. The estates of the south-west, centring on Crumlin, which constitute the largest concentration of municipal housing in Dublin, were built at this time.

Housing in the post-war period
During the wartime period, output of new housing sank to a low level and only 1,300 dwellings were built in 1946.

In 1948 a White Paper was issued containing an estimate of the number of houses needed. Despite pre-war accomplishments it was estimated that 61,000 dwellings were required, 44,500 in urban areas and the remainder in rural areas. The major problem was in Dublin where an estimated 23,500 dwellings (approximately 40 per cent of the national need) were required.

The Housing (Amendment) Acts, 1948 to 1952, provided among other things for more generous grants for private dwellings, particularly for people building dwellings for their own occupation, for higher loans to house purchasers and for the strengthening of local authority powers to deal with special housing problems. These measures had a stimulating effect on the housing programme and in the early 1950s an annual average of 14,500 dwellings were erected.

By the late 1950s, however, a downward trend was again evident. This was partly due to the belief (later found to be erroneous) that sufficient progress had been made in satisfying the need for housing throughout the country. It was also due to cutbacks in local authority capital expenditure on housing. In 1959 the report, *Economic Development*, stated:

> Private housing needs have been largely met, while local authority housing programmes have already been completed in a number of areas and are expected to be completed in all areas outside Dublin within three or four years.[4]

Between 1956 and 1958, capital expenditure on housing by public authorities was halved from £14.3 million to £7.5 million.[5] In the late 1950s the population of the Republic was falling by about 10,000 per annum, emigration was running at over 40,000 annually and some local authority housing estates were reporting vacancies. There was a dramatic rise in the number of vacancies in Dublin Corporation estates from 1954 onwards which reached a peak of well over 1,200 per annum between 1958 and 1961 and rapidly declined again later in the 1960s. Output of local authority housing in Dublin declined from a high point of 2,600 in 1951 to 279 in 1961.

In the 1960s, economic growth was accelerated and led to an upsurge in social spending. Furthermore, significant demographic changes occurred giving rise to an increased demand for housing, particularly in urban areas.

In 1964 a White Paper, *Housing: Progress and Prospects*, estimated that 50,000 dwellings were required to cater for existing needs and 8,000 for future needs. In the following year Dublin Corporation initiated the Ballymun scheme, one of the largest single housing projects in Europe at the time. The construction of over 3,000 dwellings was a formidable achievement and undoubtedly helped to alleviate housing needs in the Dublin area.

In 1969 the government issued another White Paper, *Housing in the Seventies,* which estimated that the number of dwellings required to cater for accumulated needs was 59,000, while the annual prospective need was 9,000 for the period 1966-71 and 11,500 for the mid-1970s.

During the 1960s output of housing increased steadily and in the early 1970s increased further, reaching a peak of almost 27,000 in 1975. Thereafter there was a slight decline until 1981 when almost 29,000 dwellings were built. Throughout the 1980s there was a steady decline in housing output and in 1988 the number built (15,654) was the lowest since 1971. By 1991 the figure had increased to almost 20,000. The number of dwellings completed for selected years over the past few decades is set out in Table 3.1.

Table 3.1: Output of dwellings, selected years, 1971-1991

1971	15,380
1975	26,892
1981	28,917
1985	23,948
1989	18,068
1990	19,539
1991	19,652

Source: Department of the Environment, *Bulletin of Housing Statistics*

Housing stock
The total housing stock has increased by over one-third since the end of World War I. During that period the owner occupied sector has continued to increase its share of the total stock while that of the local authority rented sector and especially the private rented sector has declined (Table 3.2). The decline of the local authority rented sector is partly accounted for by the relatively high volume of sales of dwellings to tenants which has brought them into the owner occupied sector.

Table 3.2: Tenure structure of Irish housing, 1946-1981

Sector	1946 %	1961 %	1971 %	1981 %
Owner occupied	52.7	59.8	68.8	76.1
Local authority rented	16.5	18.4	15.5	12.7
Private rented	26.1	17.2	13.3	8.1
Other	4.7	4.6	2.4	3.1
Total	100.0	100.0	100.0	100.0
Total housing stock	662,654	676,402	726,363	896,000

Factors in planning housing needs

A consideration of the principal factors affecting housing needs is a matter of concern for each local authority and for the state in general. Each housing authority is expected to ascertain the extent of the need for dwellings in its area and to assess the adequacy of the supply and prospective demand for housing.

In general, two kinds of housing needs may be recognised: accumulated or existing needs, and prospective needs. *Accumulated need* refers to the existing replacement requirements arising from the necessity (a) to replace unfit dwellings, (b) to relieve overcrowding, and (c) to provide housing for certain categories of people on medical, compassionate or other similar grounds. *Prospective need* refers to future need which can arise mainly from replacements and increase in households. One of the more important factors affecting housing needs is demographic change and, in particular, changes in household-forming age groups. In 1976 and in 1983 the NESC published reports on new dwelling needs over a period.[6] Both reports took account of prospective requirements of which the most important was the increase in the number of households. These housing projections took account not only of population growth over the period in question but also the need to eliminate overcrowding and to replace existing dwellings which were unfit for use.

Tenure sectors

In this section the salient features of the different tenure sectors (local authority, owner occupied and private rented) are outlined. The development of social housing is also addressed.

Local authority rented sector
Local authorities are mainly concerned with providing dwellings for renting to people living in unfit and over-crowded conditions and to those whose income does not allow them provide adequate accommodation for them-selves. They also provide special housing for the elderly and disabled persons.

Output of local authority housing
As a proportion of total housing output, that of local authorities has fluctuated over several decades. In 1949-50 local authority output constituted two-thirds of the total output of 8,113 dwellings. In 1989, on the other hand, local authority output accounted for only 4.3 per cent of the 18,068 dwellings built.

The stock of local authority dwellings available for renting has fluctuated over the past few decades (see Table 3.3). The fact that the stock has not increased continuously over that period is due to the sale of local authority dwellings (see pp. 57-8).

Financing
Prior to 1988 local authorities obtained loans from the local loans fund and were liable for the loan charges (interest and capital repayments). Their increasing inability to meet these charges, however, and the consequent increase in subsidy to them from the Department of the Environment to meet these charges, led to a change in

Table 3.3: Number of local authority dwellings available for renting, selected years, 1975-1990

1975	105,000
1981	104,000
1985	114,364
1988	116,270
1990	94,395*

* Provisional

January 1988. Since then, capital for the house building programme of local authorities is made by way of grants rather than fully subsidised loans.

Rents

The majority of local authority dwellings are now let on what is termed a differential rent system, i.e. a rent related to household income. The letting of dwellings at fixed rents was a feature of local authority housing in the past and the tenant's capacity to pay was not a consideration, irrespective of changes in household income. In 1934 income-related rents were introduced in Cork city, the rent being based on one-sixth of family income less certain deductions and subject to review with changes in that income. Since 1967 all new lettings of local authority dwellings throughout the country have been let on the differential rent system. For each local authority dwelling minimum and maximum rents are set and within these the tenant pays a proportion of income in rent. If household income increases, so does the rent (up to the maximum set) and if household income is reduced, so also is the rent (down to the minimum set).

Prior to 1973 differential rent schemes varied from one local authority area to another, principally in regard to allowances deductable from household income. In 1973, however, following a prolonged strike by the National Association of Tenants Organisations, a new national differential rents scheme was introduced. In effect, subsequent reviews were initiated and the terms of schemes were established by the Department of the Environment. In 1983, however, the Minister for the Environment decreed that local authorities should themselves decide on the basis of the rents schemes. Consequently there may well be differences between local authorities in the details of the schemes. In general, a complex formula is used in determining tenants' rents. The assessable income of the main income-earner (less certain allowances) is divided by a certain fraction in order to arrive at the rent. Income of other household members is also taken into account up to a certain amount.

In relation to expenditure on local authority housing it is important to note that rental income constitutes about two-thirds of the total cost of maintenance and management (Table 3.4).

Since the introduction nationally of differential rents in 1967, the proportion of local authority dwellings let on these rents has increased steadily as those on fixed rates have been phased out. By 1990 the overwhelming majority (96.2 per cent) of local authority dwellings were let on differential rents.

Table 3.4: Main elements of local authority housing finances, 1987 and 1990

	1987 £m	1990 £m
Expenditure		
Local authority and social housing	101.40	60.60
Loan charges	182.62*	–
Maintenance and management of local authority housing stock	66.19	67.28
Total	350.21	127.88
Income		
Rents	45.48	46.33
Net proceeds of sales (40% of total)	10.36	19.71
Total	55.84	66.04

*Repayments to local loans funds. From 1988 local authorities received grants from the Department of the Environment for house building purposes.

Source: Department of the Environment, *Annual Housing Statistics*

Purchase schemes
Despite the considerable output of local authority dwellings over several decades, there has not been a commensurate increase in the stock of dwellings, i.e. the total number available for letting. This is due to the fact that local authorities have operated purchase schemes to allow tenants to purchase their dwellings with a discount on the market value or replacement value of the house. By 1987 it had been estimated that of the 300,000 local authority

dwellings built since the foundation of the state, 180,000 (almost one-third of the national housing stock) had been sold to tenants.[7] Purchase schemes have been introduced from time to time to facilitate this process, the terms of the purchase scheme varying and having a definite time limit for take up. In 1988 a purchase scheme was introduced which allowed 40 per cent discount on the market value of a local authority dwelling (50 per cent in the case of those built prior to 1961), together with a £2,000 grant available to purchasers of new houses. This scheme is estimated to result in the sale of approximately 30,000 local authority dwellings, thus reducing the stock available for letting to about 90,000.

The sale of local authority dwellings over a period of time has helped to account for the high proportion of owner occupied dwellings but it is a system which has met with some criticism. On the one hand it is argued that the capacity of local authorities to meet housing needs would be improved in the long run if much less of the stock was sold to tenants and if such sales were at less generous discounts. On the other hand it is argued that the sale of local authority dwellings encourages better maintenance and improvement of individual dwellings and therefore of the housing stock; it provides a pool of reasonably priced houses suitable to the needs of first-time purchasers and reduces the maintenance and management burden on the local authorities.[8] Since rents meet only a small proportion of the total housing costs for local authorities it has even been suggested that it would make financial sense for the state to give away the entire local authority stock to the tenants free of charge and actually save money in the process.[9]

Priority in letting of dwellings
Prior to the passing of the 1988 Housing Act, local authorities had to establish a scheme of priority in the letting of dwellings so that families or persons most in need of housing received prompt attention. Overall priority was given to families living in dangerous premises, families which became homeless through emergency situations such as fire or flood, families which required housing on medical grounds, and families evicted or displaced from areas required for redevelopment.

Some local authorities had to operate a points system in order to establish priority. In practice this would have occurred in the large urban areas. The highest number of points were generally allocated to those families living in unfit or overcrowded dwellings. Over the past few decades approximately half of new dwellings let by local authorities annually were to families living in overcrowded conditions.

Under the 1988 Housing Act, local authorities are obliged to assess the extent of need for local authority accommodation and to revise their scheme of letting priorities. The aim of the scheme of priorities is to ensure equal opportunity for different categories of need in relation to housing accommodation. The 1988 Housing Act stipulated that the needs of homeless persons should be provided for and in order to ensure equality of treatment a local authority can set aside a proportion of the dwellings becoming available for letting to particular categories of people, including homeless persons.

During the period 1981-88 the total number of households on local authority waiting lists fell from 27,00 to 17,700.[10] This accounts in part for the decline in capital expenditure on local authority housing and the decline in output of local authority dwellings. In 1989 there was an upturn in the numbers on the waiting lists and the first assessment of housing needs under the 1988 Housing Act indicated that 19,400 households (including homeless and travellers) were qualified for local authority housing. Within two years another assessment showed a further increase in the number of such households (Table 3.5). More than half (55 per cent) of the households deemed to be in need of housing were living in unfit dwellings, overcrowded dwellings, or were sharing involuntarily with other households. The greatest proportionate increases by category over the two-year period were among the disabled, the homeless and households unable to afford existing accommodation.

Owner occupied sector

By comparison with other European countries Ireland has a relatively high proportion of owner occupiers. This is due to a number of factors. Chief among these are historical and cultural factors and the schemes of state aid to the owner occupier.

Table 3.5: Assessment of housing needs, 1989 and 1991

Category	1989	1991	% change
Households:			
In unfit dwellings	4,324	4,590	6.1
In overcrowded dwellings	4,621	5,896	27.6
Sharing involuntarily with			
other households	2,000	2,432	21.6
In institutional care	156	–	–
In need of housing on medical/			
compassionate grounds	1,187	1,331	12.1
Unable to afford existing			
accommodation	2,809	4,075	45.1
Young persons leaving			
institutional care or without			
family accommodation	–	104	–
Homeless	987	1,507	52.7
Travellers	834	748	–10.3
Elderly	2,349	2,379	1.3
Disabled	108	180	66.6
Total	19,376	23,242	20.0

Source: Department of the Environment, *A Plan for Social Housing* (1991); Department of the Environment, *Annual Housing Statistics*

It has been suggested that the legacy of the land reform measures in the late nineteenth century and early decades of the present century influence the pattern of owner occupation.[11] During that period farmers, who had been tenants of their land, became owner occupiers.

While it is difficult to measure the extent of the influence of cultural factors on the level of owner occupation in Ireland, there is little doubt that the state has also contributed to Ireland's relatively high proportion of owner occupiers by a system of financial aid, part of which originated in the latter part of the nineteenth century. This system includes grants and loans provided by local authorities and income tax relief on the interest element of mortgages.

Grants
Since the introduction of grants for the provision of new dwellings in 1919, the grants levels have been increased on

several occasions and the system has been altered to respond to the needs of particular sections of the community. In July 1977, for example, all previous grant schemes (state and local authority) were rescinded and a new £1,000 grant for first-time purchasers of new houses was introduced. In 1985 this grant was increased to £2,000 and this is the level of grant which is still in force. Other forms of grants have been made available in recent years, the mortgage subsidy scheme for example, and a surrender grant of £5,000 available to local authority tenants who moved into the private sector to purchase a dwelling.

The provision of grants for new dwellings has undoubtedly helped people to meet the costs of buying or providing a house but it has also provided a stimulus to the production of houses. In fact it can be argued that the grants system was designed as much to help the building industry as to help persons to acquire houses of their own.

Grants have also been provided from time to time by the state for the reconstruction and improvement of existing houses. These grants have usually operated for certain defined periods. The most recent scheme was introduced in 1985 but was terminated in 1987.

Income tax relief
The interest element of a mortgage is allowable against income tax, subject to certain limits. This concession to house purchasers is a consequence of the income tax code and was not intended as a specific housing subsidy. At one stage tax relief was available on all forms of interest but in 1982 it was confined to housing purposes. The actual savings in tax remission will depend on the marginal rate at which the person pays tax. Persons on the highest rates of tax, therefore, will benefit most substantially from the income tax relief.

Other aids
Apart from the grants and the system of tax relief there are a number of other means designed to help owner occupation. Thus, for example, there is no stamp duty payable on a new house for which a state grant is payable. In the case of second-hand houses, however, there is a liability for stamp duty.

Financing of private housing

Apart from state and local authority investment in housing, a number of other agencies are involved in the provision of house purchase loans. Of these, the building societies have played the most important role. Up to relatively recently, assurance companies also had a substantial role to play but that declined considerably throughout the 1970s and their contribution in this area is now almost negligible. In the supplementary budget of 1975, the Minister for Finance directed the associated banks to provide house purchase loans totalling £40 million over the following two years. This directive was intended to provide a stimulus to the construction industry during a difficult period, as well as providing an additional source of loans to the house purchaser. The banks, while exceeding the figure stipulated by the Minister, have continued to provide beyond this period and they are now an important source of finance for house purchasers (Table 3.6). Up to recently local authorities have also been an important source of finance especially for persons on low or relatively low incomes, but their role has declined sharply in this area since the 1970s.

Private rented sector

There has been a constant decline in the dwellings available for private renting in Ireland. Up to 1982, a distinction could be made within the private rented sector between two categories, i.e. dwellings whose rents were controlled (restricted) and those whose rents were uncontrolled

Table 3.6: Number of house purchase loans paid for new and other houses by main agencies, selected years, 1971-1991

	Building societies	Local authorities	Associated banks	Assurance companies	Other agencies	Total
1971	6,665 (56.8%)	3,213 (27.4%)	– –	1,850 (15.8%)	– –	11,728 (100%)
1979	14,783 (59.7%)	6,943 (28.1%)	2,494 (10.1%)	522 (2.1%)	–	24,742 (100%)
1991	17,965 (53.3%)	1,278 (3.8%)	9,888 (29.3%)	–	4,589 (13.6%)	33,720 (100%)

Source: Department of the Environment, *Annual Housing Statistics*

(unrestricted). While the rents of tenants in uncontrolled dwellings were largely determined by market forces, rents were controlled for certain dwellings under the Rent Restrictions Acts, 1960 and 1967. The categories of dwellings excluded from rent control were complex but, for example, all furnished lettings and dwellings built since 1941 were excluded.

In 1982 the High Court ruled that sections of the Rent Restrictions Acts were unconstitutional. This decision was appealed to the Supreme Court which upheld the decision of the High Court. As a result of this, the government was obliged to introduce the Housing Act of 1982 in order to protect the interests of tenants in dwellings which had been subject to rent control. The Act provided for security of tenure for existing tenants and also provided a mechanism by which the rents could be reviewed. If landlord and tenant agreed on any increase in rent then there would not be any intervention by the state; otherwise the rent could be established by a district court. For various reasons, this court system was found to be unsatisfactory and rent tribunals were established in 1983 to perform this function.

In order to avoid any hardship which could arise for tenants faced with a substantial increase in rent following decontrol, the Department of Social Welfare introduced a rent allowance scheme. This allowance was confined to tenants in the former rent controlled dwellings, subject to a means test, and the maximum allowance is the difference between the old and the new rent. In 1991 there were 1,004 recipients of this allowance and the cost to the Department of Social Welfare was £878,000.

Unlike the local authority and owner occupier sectors, there are few subsidies available to those in the private rented sector. Apart from the rent allowance scheme administered by the Department of Social Welfare described above, assistance with rent may be provided under the supplementary welfare allowance scheme and tax relief on rent is allowed for persons aged fifty-five or over. In addition, it has been stated that:

> The Irish private rented sector remains virtually unregulated; its tenants are afforded less protection than any other such group in Europe – and less state subsidies.[12]

For some time, Threshold, a voluntary organisation providing a service for those in the private rented sector, has
pointed to the lack of state policy in this area. In 1982 it
published *Private Rented: The Forgotten Sector*,[13] and it has
consistently argued, for example, that tenants should have
greater security of tenure and that minimum standards of
accommodation should be introduced.

In response to these demands, the *Programme for Economic
and Social Progress* (PESP) (1991) indicated that the position
regarding tenants in the private rented sector was being
reviewed and that the government proposed to introduce
safeguards for tenants on completion of this review.[14] In this
context it should be noted that a number of local authorities
had enacted byelaws under the 1966 Housing Act laying
down minimum standards for rented housing.

In line with the commitment in the PESP additional safeguards for tenants in regard to such matters as rent books,
standards of accommodation and notice to quit were provided for in the Housing (Miscellaneous Provisions) Act of
1992.[15]

Social housing
In recent years attention has begun to be focused on the
issue of accommodation for persons with special needs,
such as the elderly and the handicapped. This particular
type of housing need has been largely met by organisations
and housing associations providing housing on a non-profit
basis. It has been pointed out that Ireland has not shared in
the development of the social housing movement which
has characterised many European countries over the past
few decades and that state support for social housing
organisations has been a peripheral aspect of housing
policy.[16]

In 1984 the Department of the Environment introduced
a scheme – the capital assistance scheme for non-profit and
voluntary housing – to assist approved voluntary housing
associations with the capital funding cost of housing
projects for certain categories of persons with special
housing needs. Under the scheme, 80 per cent of the
capital cost in building or renovating a property for accommodation in self-contained units for the elderly and

handicapped was provided. Subsequently, the scheme was extended to include projects for homeless persons and the level of funding was also increased. With this assistance a number of housing units have been provided by different organisations within the past decade. Examples include HAIL (Housing Association for Integrated Living) and Focus Housing Association, which have provided units for homeless and socially vulnerable persons such as those who have left hospital. While capital assistance is available to social housing organisations, they are responsible for the ongoing running costs such as maintenance, management and social support. The Housing Centre functions as an advisory body for new housing associations or voluntary organisations wishing to develop a housing service.

Homelessness
While there are differences as to the precise definition of homelessness it is generally agreed that the extent of the problem has increased in Ireland in recent decades. The plight of the homeless has been highlighted by the Simon Community and other groups who have campaigned for greater action and legislation. Confusion existed as to which state agency (health board or local authority) had statutory responsibility for providing accommodation for the homeless. In 1983 Senator Brendan Ryan introduced a Homeless Persons Bill in the Seanad in order to bring greater clarity into the situation. However, the government opposed his Bill and introduced its own in 1985. This lapsed when the Dáil was dissolved in January 1987.

In 1988 the Housing Act was passed with two main objectives:

- to revive and update the statutory basis for the provision, improvement, management and letting of local authority housing, so as to ensure that the needs of categories of persons such as the homeless, the aged, the disabled and travellers get due priority, and
- to increase the powers of housing authorities in regard to the accommodation of homeless persons.

The Act did not place a statutory duty on a local authority

to provide accommodation for homeless persons but it did empower them either on their own or in conjunction with other agencies to provide a range of suitable accommodation. Guidelines were issued by the Department of the Environment which encouraged local authorities to operate the new powers available to them in a flexible and sensitive manner and these guidelines stressed the desirability of planning, liaison and consultation with health boards and voluntary organisations in implementing the Act. Within a relatively short time it became clear that some local authorities were either unwilling or unable because of lack of finance to comply with these guidelines. By 1991 the impasse still remained and in the PESP it was agreed that:

> Special steps will be taken by the Department of the Environment to ensure the full implementation both in the letter and the spirit by local authorities of the guidelines.[17]

The lack of response to implementing the guidelines was criticised in *A Plan for Social Housing* and it indicated that steps would be taken by the Minister for the Environment to prevail on local authorities to utilise fully their powers under the Housing Act of 1988 to secure accommodation for homeless persons.[18]

Quality of housing
A general indication of quality of housing stock and housing conditions may be obtained by reference to the age of dwellings, the degree of overcrowding and the presence of basic amenities.[19]

There is a broad correlation between age and fitness of dwellings. A relatively high proportion of dwellings in Ireland have been built within the past few decades. Consequently the proportion of the housing stock built before 1919 has declined considerably (from 45 per cent in 1971 to 29 per cent in 1981).

If overcrowding is defined as two or more persons per room then the improvement here has been substantial. In 1926 over one-third (37.1 per cent) of the population lived in overcrowded conditions, but by 1981 this had declined to 1 in 17 (5.9 per cent). Related to this has been the decline in the average household size from 4.48 in 1926 to

3.68 in 1981. Over the same period the average number of persons per room in private households declined from 1.19 to 0.74.

Similarly, there has been a dramatic improvement in the proportion of dwellings with basic amenities, such as piped water supply, from 38.7 per cent in 1946 to 95 per cent in 1981. A considerable disparity existed here until recently between urban and rural areas with the latter lagging far behind. Part of the reason for this, however, is the fact that it was more difficult and costly to provide schemes in rural areas with a scattered settlement pattern than in high density urban areas. During the 1970s in particular with the expansion of group water schemes the disparity between rural and urban areas was reduced. The same type of disparity between areas existed up to recently in relation to electricity. By 1981, however, 98.9 per cent of all dwellings had electricity as compared with 83 per cent in 1961.

Despite the improvement in housing conditions a NESC report in 1988 concluded that:

> ... certain groups have benefited little, or not at all, from the general improvement in housing conditions over the past decade or so. This is indicated by the stagnation, or even deterioration, in housing conditions which has occurred among those with the poorest quality of dwellings or with none at all. There has been an increasing disparity between the quality of housing services enjoyed by most households, and those obtained by those at the bottom end of the housing market.[20]

Among the evidence given in support of the above was a reference to the situation in some local authority estates in certain urban areas, which are characterised by a combination of poor community facilities, lack of accessibility to jobs and shopping, poorly maintained fabric and design problems which have led to difficulties with security and vandalism.

Housing policy
It is only within the past two decades that housing policy has been subjected to critical analysis. In 1977, for example, the NESC published a report on housing subsidies. This was the first attempt to quantify the value of subsidies, both

explicit (e.g. grants) and implicit (e.g. income tax relief on interest element of mortgage) to the various sectors within the housing system. The report estimated that in 1975 the highest subsidy on a household basis went to those who purchased their local authority dwellings.[21] In that year the average household subsidy varied little between owner occupier and local authority tenant.

Baker and O'Brien, in 1979, presented an excellent overview of the housing system with reference to efficiency and equity.[22] They argued that while the system was tolerably efficient at providing accommodation, it was also seriously unfair in that it favoured those who already own or rent houses at the expense of those seeking housing. They referred to the wide variation in the quality of dwellings and housing costs within each tenure. Some of their recommendations for improvements have been implemented since then, the greater availability of local authority housing for single persons, for example, and the abolition of rent control.

In 1981 Blackwell argued that most elements of housing policy do not work to the achievement of either *horizontal* or *vertical* equity.[23] By horizontal equity is meant that households with broadly similar income and household characteristics (e.g. family size) should obtain equal net benefits from the system. Vertical equity is concerned with the implications of policy for those who are not equal and with the extent to which there is a transfer of resources in a progressive manner, i.e. that those on the lowest income should benefit most. In relation to horizontal equity Blackwell pointed out, for example, that there is a considerable difference in benefit between those purchasing new houses (where both grants and stamp duty exemption apply) and those purchasing second-hand houses. The most obvious form of public housing policy which does not accord with vertical equity is the tax relief available on the interest element of a mortgage. This favours people on the highest incomes with the highest rates of marginal tax; the tax relief is greater at this level.

While there have been various criticisms of elements of housing policy and while a number of adjustments to policy have been made in response to these, a few key areas are being constantly highlighted.

Firstly, in addition to the stated objectives, housing policy is designed to help the building industry. This is exemplified by the fact that grants for first-time purchasers are confined to new houses only. Furthermore, various schemes have been introduced from time to time to provide a boost to the building industry, e.g. the home improvement grants scheme (introduced in 1985, abolished in 1987) and the builders' grants for new dwellings (introduced in 1986, abolished in 1987).

Secondly, there is increasing concern that the secondary objective of housing policy, i.e. the promotion of owner occupation, has been pursued to the detriment of those on the fringes of the housing system and not, therefore, in a position to benefit from the public subsidies available. Now that four-fifths of dwellings are owner occupied it is argued that greater attention should be focused on marginal groups and the needs of those in the private rented sector.

The NESC in various reports has consistently questioned the validity of existing policy and has argued for a more balanced housing strategy. In its most recent report, the NESC has stated:

> The central thrust of housing policy has always been the encouragement of owner occupation. In the Council's view, owner occupation *per se* should not be an end in itself, but one of a series of instruments to achieve the goal of adequate housing, in an acceptable environment, at an affordable price or rent.[24]

The NESC argued that it is necessary to achieve a better balance between tenures and that, while owner occupation remains the main tenure, the other tenures (local authority, private rented and voluntary/social housing) should play an appropriate role. This should be the fundamental aim of housing policy. The key points in the NESC's housing strategy are as follows:

- an equitable and efficient tax/subsidy regime for owner occupied housing entailing a property tax, full mortgage interest tax relief at the standard rate, and capital gains tax on real gains from sales of dwellings
- a greater emphasis throughout the housing system as a whole on maintenance, refurbishment and renewal

- an explicit policy for the private rented sector which sustains demand for this tenure, encourages supply and provides a modicum of regulation (but not rent regulation)
- a more sophisticated policy for local authority housing, incorporating a more equitable and efficient rent system, better maintenance and management and a much more restrictive use of discount sales of dwellings
- a greater commitment to the voluntary, social and cooperative sectors
- a locally coordinated resettlement strategy for the homeless and those with acute housing needs.

Some of the criticisms made by the NESC and others have been responded to in part by the Minister for the Environment in *A Plan for Social Housing* published in February 1991. While reiterating the broad objective of housing policy as enunciated by successive governments and quoted at the beginning of this chapter, the Plan goes on to indicate that future strategy will include (a) promoting owner occupation as a form of tenure preferred by most people; (b) developing and implementing responses appropriate to changing social housing needs; (c) mitigating the extent and effects of social segregation in housing.

The Plan indicated a number of policy changes. In relation to local authority housing, for example, it indicated that the approach of local authorities would be broader and more diverse than its traditional role. The new measures envisaged for local authorities would include the following:

- to avoid building large housing estates which have 'reinforced social segregation with adverse consequences'
- to purchase private houses or existing houses in need of refurbishment where it is more economic than building new houses
- to carry out improvements to existing local authority dwellings as opposed to providing new houses
- to introduce a system of shared ownership with tenants in which the local authority would take a 50 per cent share
- to introduce a new mortgage allowance (over five years) for tenants moving to private houses.

The *Plan for Social Housing* also contained proposals for initiatives in relation to homeless and travelling people, voluntary and cooperative housing, home ownership and, as already indicated, the private rented sector. The *Plan for Social Housing* could be described as the most comprehensive government statement on housing in recent decades and was a response to the changing housing needs in society. It addressed the key issues which had been of concern for some time, proposed initiatives in all sectors and while it did nothing to alter the predominant position of owner occupation it nevertheless involved fundamental changes in policy. The legislative base for these changes was provided for in the Housing (Miscellaneous Provisions) Act of 1992.

4

Education

Introduction

In many respects the system of education in Ireland is highly complex. Education is carried out at three levels and considerable variation exists not only between these levels but within them. The management and financing of first and second level schools are different and at first level there are different kinds of primary schools, while at second level there are four distinct sub-sections. Despite the fact that there is substantial state support at all levels, there are few state schools in the accepted sense. The influence of the churches (especially Catholic) on the development of the system is profound at all levels.

The present system represents a curious mixture of state and church interests, particularly at first level and in some parts of second level. Secondary schools, for example, are in receipt of various state subsidies yet are privately owned and managed. Apart from the churches, there are various other interest groups, such as teachers' unions and parents' organisations. The presence of these groups, coupled with the fact that there is little legislative basis for education, means that it is often difficult to obtain agreement on policy changes. The following pages will illustrate this.

Since the mid-1960s some important changes have occurred in the education system. These include the introduction of free post-primary education and the establishment of new institutions such as comprehensive and community schools at second level and regional technical colleges at third level. These innovations have been accompanied by an increase in the population and increased participation rates at all levels. All this has involved greater public expenditure and almost inevitably, owing to budgetary constraints in recent years, questions have been raised about the appropriate allocation of resources at the various levels of education.

The main features of each of these levels and adult education are considered in this chapter. Some key issues in education are also considered.

First level education

Origins of present system[1]
Many basic features of modern Irish primary or first level education can be traced back to the National Board of Education, established in 1831. Prior to that there was no uniform system of primary education and while some areas were well served by schools others had only rudimentary forms of schooling.[2] A number of organisations promoted first level education in the early decades of the nineteenth century, for example, the Kildare Place Society and Catholic religious orders.

In 1831 the British House of Commons voted a sum of £30,000 towards primary education in Ireland. This money was to be administered by the National Board of Education which consisted of seven commissioners representing the main religious denominations. The Board was given power to contribute to the cost of building schools, pay inspection costs, contribute to teachers' salaries, establish model schools and provide school books. The system was to provide for 'combined moral, literary and separate religious education'. It was decided that schools run by religious orders were to be given the same assistance as other schools, provided they complied with the rules of the Board.

The Board's early success was hindered by opposition and lack of cooperation. In 1837, for example, the Irish Christian Brothers withdrew their schools from connection with the Board. Four years later, however, Pope Gregory XVI encouraged Catholics to support the national schools. While some of the Catholic hierarchy welcomed the new system others, notably Dr John MacHale, Archbishop of Tuam, were less enthusiastic and forbade their clergy to cooperate with the Board.

The training of teachers for the national schools proved to be another contentious issue. In 1837, the Board established a training school and three model schools at Marlborough Street, Dublin. Teachers were to be trained on the principle of the 'mixed system', i.e. children of all denominations would be taught and religious and secular instruction would not be separate. The Catholic hierarchy forbade their clerical managers to appoint teachers trained in the model schools to schools under their control. In 1883 the Board decided to recognise denominational training colleges and two Catholic colleges (St Patrick's, Drumcondra, for men and Our Lady of Mercy, Blackrock, for women) were established in Dublin. A Church of Ireland training college for men and women was affiliated to the Board in the following year. Three other training colleges at Waterford (1891), Belfast (1900), and Limerick (1907), were established.

Notwithstanding the limitations and somewhat tempestuous history of the national system, it could claim credit for considerable achievements by 1922 when the Commissioners of the National Board of Education were replaced by a branch of the newly-founded Department of Education under an Irish Minister for Education.[3] Perhaps the most important consequence of the national system was that it was the chief means by which the country was transformed from one in which illiteracy predominated into one in which most people could read and write: in 1841 over half the population (53 per cent) aged five years and over could neither read nor write, and by 1901 this proportion had declined to 14 per cent. In the eradication of mass illiteracy, therefore, credit must be given to the national system. The system also ensured that national schools were established in all parts of the country. The number of schools increased from just over 1,000 in 1834 to almost 8,000 in 1921, and the school-going population increased from 107,000 in 1833 to 685,000 in 1891. This occurred despite a decline of over 50 per cent in the total population between 1841 and 1921.

One of the main objectives of the National Board of Education, the establishment of non-denominational schools, was not achieved. The state system of non-denominational education established in 1831 had become, by the time the Irish state was founded, a system of denominational education and has remained so ever since. In fact, as stated in the *Rules for National Schools under the Department of Education* (1965), the state gives explicit recognition to the denominational character of these schools.

Compulsory schooling
Under the Irish Education Act, 1892, attendance on at least seventy-five days in each half year was made compulsory for children between the ages of six and fourteen. A number of acceptable excuses for non-attendance were specified by the Act, e.g. sickness, harvesting operations, fishing, any other unavoidable cause, or in cases where the child was already receiving suitable elementary education. Initially the application of the Act was limited to municipal boroughs and towns but in 1898 it was extended to all parts of the country. The enforcement of the Act was particularly difficult in rural areas. School attendance committees set up by local authorities helped to enforce the law but not all local authorities set up such committees.

While the Act may not have had the desired effect, it nevertheless brought about a change in school attendance. In 1902 the average yearly attendance was 63 per cent and this increased to 76 per cent by 1908.

The School Attendance Act, 1926, made further provisions for the enforcement of compulsory schooling and remains the main statute governing school attendance. An amendment in 1972 raised the school leaving age to fifteen years.

Management and finance
Initially, the National Board of Education was willing to give special consideration to any joint applications for aid from members of different religious denominations within a parish. What happened in practice was that where there were sufficient numbers of children of different denominations then the Catholic or non-Catholic clergy or members of religious orders applied for separate aid in building a school. The pupils, therefore, were concentrated in separate schools under local clerical or religious order management. This was the beginning of the managerial system, which survived up to 1975.

Ironically, while the direct administration of primary schools and the appointment and dismissal of teachers has remained in the hands of local managers, the state has always paid a large share of the cost of building schools and pays the teachers' salaries in full. The non-state character of the school has been preserved by the provision of a site from local funds together with a local contribution towards the cost of building the school. The state also contributes towards the maintenance of schools. The situation in relation to the subsidy for school buildings has been summarised as follows:

> While in theory the state contributes two-thirds of the approved cost of a primary school building, this contribution is open to negotiation, and in the vast majority of cases is very much higher. The system is not entirely satisfactory, since the amount of the state grant provided often depends on the case put forward in respect of local circumstances.[4]

There are eighty-five private primary schools and these do not receive any state subsidy and are totally financed by parents' fees.

In practice a distinction can be made between primary schools. The majority are referred to as ordinary national schools and are mainly under either Roman Catholic or Protestant clerical patronage. Schools run by religious orders are referred to as Roman Catholic monastery (male orders) or convent (female orders) schools. In addition there are special schools for physically and mentally handicapped children and schools in which the curriculum is taught wholly or mainly through the medium of Irish. There is also a small number of model national schools directly under the control of the Department of Education.

While suggestions were made in the early 1970s to involve parents and teachers formally in school management, little became of these until the world oil crisis of 1973-74 presented the opportunity. The soaring cost of heating oil meant that the state would have to substantially increase its maintenance subsidy to primary schools, otherwise the burden would fall on the local community. In October 1974, the Minister for Education, Richard Burke, announced a new scheme of state aid towards the maintenance costs of primary schools. Instead of paying schools a proportion of the maintenance costs, a capitation grant of

£6 per pupil (to be matched by an amount equivalent to one-quarter of the state grant to be collected locally) would be given only to those schools which had set up joint management committees by October 1975, composed of four nominees of the patron and two parents. The Minister subsequently indicated that teachers should also be represented on these committees. Schools which had not set up the committees would have to accept a lower subsidy from the Department of Education towards the upkeep of their schools. From a financial viewpoint, therefore, it was in the manager's interest to establish committees. The manner in which management boards were introduced in primary schools has been aptly described as a form of 'gentle blackmail'.[5] It also illustrates the difficulty of making policy changes in the Irish education system. In the absence of a legislative basis, change was introduced by agreement among the various interests involved rather than by legislation. In this instance, a financial carrot achieved in one year something which in all probability would have taken several years to achieve.

While the principle of teacher and parental representation on management boards was accepted, in practice protracted negotiations between the main interests (Irish National Teachers' Organisation, the Catholic hierarchy, the Department of Education and the Catholic Primary School Managers' Association) took place before agreement to establish committees was reached and before the exact functions and composition of the boards of management were agreed. It was not until November 1976 that the constitution and rules of procedure for the management boards were published. Following further negotiations, these rules and the composition of boards were subsequently altered in 1981. In schools of seven teachers or more, the board is comprised of a total of ten members, i.e. six nominees of the patron, two parents elected by other parents, a principal teacher and one other teacher elected by teaching staff.

The patron of the school appoints the chairman of the board. For national schools, the bishop or archbishop (Catholic or non-Catholic) is normally the patron. The boards are responsible for the maintenance of the school and the collection of the local contribution (which must not be a levy on parents). The Review Body on Primary Education received submissions which were critical of the management system, e.g. the Department of Education decides on all major matters of policy; the patron plays a central role in the appointment of the board, the chairperson, the principal and assistant teachers; and agreements between trade unions and the Department limit further the autonomy of the board. Having considered alternative proposals the Review Body did not recommend any change in the composition of the boards. Instead it recommended that the future of the boards be reappraised and strengthened, e.g. that they be given greater autonomy in relation to many matters which at present require the approval of the Department of Education.[6]

In 1990/91 the Department of Education grant was £28 per pupil and the local contribution £7 (a total of £35 per pupil). Any additional finances required have to be raised by the board of management.

Rationalisation

A relatively high density of population in the mid-nineteenth century, combined with the fact that education was based on the parish, encouraged the building of small primary schools serving a rather limited catchment area. As population declined throughout the latter part of the nineteenth and first half of the present century, however, many schools, particularly those in rural areas, became vulnerable to closure. Since its establishment, the Department of Education had sought to amalgamate those schools which had the smallest number of pupils. In many areas there was considerable opposition to school closures, reflecting the value of the school as a focal point in the local community.

The *Investment in Education* report (1965) indicated that on a cost-effective basis the one-teacher and two-teacher primary schools were inefficient, for example, in the range of subjects taught and in the rate of pupils' progress through school.[7] This report influenced subsequent policy towards small schools and an intensive programme of primary school rationalisation was embarked upon. Within a decade (between 1967 and 1977), 471 one-teacher and 1,186 two-teacher schools were closed or amalgamated.

During the same period the total number of primary schools fell from 4,625 to 3,372. In 1967, one-teacher and two-teacher schools accounted for almost two-thirds of all primary schools; by 1990, the proportion had fallen to one-quarter (Table 4.1). It should be noted that while small rural schools were being closed or amalgamated others were being established in the expanding urban areas.

Table 4.1: Number of small schools and total number of schools at primary level* 1967-1990

	1967	1977	1990
(a) Number of one- and two-teacher schools	2,920	1,263	844
(b) Total number of primary schools	4,625	3,372	3,235
(c) (a) as % of (b)	63.1	37.4	26.0

* Special schools for handicapped children are not included.

Source: Department of Education, *Statistical Report*

A NESC report published in 1976 questioned the efficacy of closing small rural schools and referred to the trend in Scandinavian countries, especially Norway, where the process of rationalisation had been reversed.[8] In February 1977, the Minister for Education, Peter Barry, in his first major policy statement since taking office two months previously, made an announcement that the Department of Education would no longer force the amalgamation of small schools into larger units.[9]

Denominationalism and primary schools
It has already been noted that despite the intentions of the National Board of Education to establish a non-denominational school structure, what emerged was a system of denominational schools. The preface to the *Rules for National Schools under the Department of Education* (1965) gives recognition to such schools:

> ... the state provides for free primary education for children in national schools, and gives explicit recognition to the denominational character of these schools.[10]

In the mid-1970s a movement to establish multi-denominational schools was initiated by some parents in parts of Dublin. The Department of Education was uncooperative while the Catholic Church opposed the concept. Gradually the movement was afforded recognition and state financial support for the establishment of schools was provided. The first multi-denominational school to open was the Dalkey School Project (Dublin) in 1978. By 1991 there were ten such schools (six in the Dublin region).

The policy in relation to multi-denominational schools has been outlined in the *Programme for Action, 1984-87*:

> Where the government is convinced that the establishment of a multi-denominational school represents the clear wishes of parents in an area and where such schools can be provided on a viable basis, support will be given to such developments on the same terms which would be available for the establishment of schools under denominational patronage.[11]

Second level education
Second level education is conducted mainly in four types of schools – secondary, vocational, comprehensive and community. Since the origins, financing, ownership and management structure of these schools differ, each will be examined separately in this section.

Secondary schools
While state aid was made available for primary education in 1831 it was not made available for secondary education until 1878 and even then the level of aid was comparatively small. Under the Intermediate Education Act, 1878, the secondary school education system in its present form took shape. The Act established the Intermediate Education Board with seven commissioners to administer funds for examination purposes. The word 'intermediate' was taken to imply a system of education between elementary or primary instruction and higher education. Junior, middle and senior grade examinations were established under the Act and results fees were paid to the managers of schools in which candidates passed the examinations. The principal means of obtaining state aid, therefore, was through success in

examinations. On the credit side, the new system imposed a uniform curriculum on secondary schools where variety had predominated. Since aid available from the state was limited, however, schools relied heavily on students' fees to meet capital and current costs. Unlike the primary school system whereby schools could be established in practically every area with state support, the distribution of secondary schools was mainly confined to urban areas. Consequently, many areas of the country lacked secondary schools, the greatest concentration being in the Dublin area and along the east coast generally, while few existed in the province of Connacht.

The Intermediate Education Board was dissolved in 1922 and in 1925 its functions were taken over by the Department of Education. Under the Intermediate Education (Amendment) Act, 1924, the system of paying grants to schools on the results of public examinations was discontinued. Instead, capitation grants were paid to schools for pupils over twelve years of age who followed prescribed courses and who made a certain number of attendances (130 days during the school year). The initial grant was £7 per junior pupil and £10 per senior pupil.

In 1924 the junior, middle and senior grade examinations were replaced by the intermediate and leaving certificate examinations. In 1925, the first year of the new examination system, 2,903 pupils sat for the intermediate certificate examination and 995 for the leaving certificate (these numbers had increased to 60,394 and 55,641 respectively by 1991).

Incremental salaries for recognised secondary teachers were introduced in 1925 in schools which fulfilled certain conditions regarding size and staffing ratio.

Finance
The government of the Free State recognised the private ownership of all secondary schools and decided to give neither building nor maintenance grants but to help them indirectly by means of capitation grants. An opportunity was therefore lost of redressing the serious imbalance in the distribution of secondary schools. It was not until 1965 that state capital grants were made available for secondary schools. Under this scheme, capital grants of 70 per cent of

the cost of building the school or an extension were made available and the present level is 80 per cent. Where a loan is borrowed from a source other than the Department of Education, 80 per cent of the annual repayments (capital and interest) are paid by the Department. Alternatively, the Department may pay the total cost of the building, 20 per cent being repayable by the school authorities over a fifteen-year period.

Up to 1986, the current expenditure of secondary schools was subsidised by:

• a capitation grant (the amount varying according to the number of senior and junior pupils as well as attendance during the previous school year), and
• a supplemental grant in lieu of fees charged by schools participating in the free post-primary education scheme introduced in 1967-68.

In 1986 these two grants were combined into a capitation grant based on enrolment. The value of the capitation grant in 1990-91 was £150.

The subsidy for Protestant secondary education is organised on a different basis. The majority of the Protestant secondary schools are not in the free scheme and the Department of Education pays a block grant to the Secondary Education Committee which distributes it, in accordance with a means test, to Protestant parents in order to subsidise their children's attendance at Protestant schools.[12]

Management
Secondary schools are privately owned and managed, the majority by Catholic religious orders and a minority by Catholic or Protestant laymen or foundations. The regulations of the Department of Education require that schools in receipt of state grants employ a certain minimum number of registered teachers and pay each of these teachers, if a lay teacher, a fixed minimum basic salary of £400. In addition to this basic salary, an incremental salary is paid by the Department of Education to recognised teachers.

In recent years management boards, consisting of

parents, teachers and representatives of religious orders, have been established in a number of schools.

Free post-primary education scheme
One of the more significant findings of the *Investment in Education* report (1965) was that there were serious inequalities in the numbers from different socio-economic groups in post-primary schools; in particular, the report showed that only 29.1 per cent were the children of semi-skilled and unskilled workers, while 70.2 per cent were the children of professionals, employers, managers and senior salaried employees.[13]

The introduction of the free post-primary education scheme in 1967-68 was an attempt to ensure equality of access to all seeking education beyond first level. Prior to this, entrance to secondary schools in general depended as much on ability to pay fees as intellectual capacity. It must also be noted, however, that while all secondary schools charged fees prior to the introduction of the scheme, ability to pay fees was not a condition of entry to some schools managed by religious orders. In effect, they operated a free scheme for pupils from low income families long before the Department of Education took the initiative.

Under the scheme, secondary schools which opted to discontinue charging school fees for pupils would be paid a supplemental grant per pupil equal to the fee charged in the school year 1966-67. The majority of secondary schools agreed to participate in the free scheme.

The free post-primary education scheme also provided for grants towards free school books and accessories for necessitous day pupils. Under the scheme, free transport was also provided for pupils living more than three miles from a school in which free education was available.

A limited scheme of free post-primary education had been under consideration in the Department of Education during the 1960s and it was intended that such a scheme be introduced in 1970 to coincide with the raising of the school leaving age to fifteen years. That the scheme was introduced earlier than planned for was due to the Minister for Education, Donogh O'Malley. Seán O'Connor, Assistant Secretary in the Department of Education at the time, has recounted that:

We, the planners, prepared to introduce free education in tandem with the raising of the school leaving age in 1970 and all our urging and striving for coordination and cooperation had that year as a focal point ... I have long been convinced that had matters proceeded according to our plans, when 1970 came, free education would not have been on the agenda at all, or if it had been, it would have been in such attenuated form as scarce to merit the title. Donogh O'Malley shattered our plans and left Ireland in his debt.[14]

The numbers participating in second level education rose dramatically in the decade following the introduction of free post-primary education. Some of this, however, was due to the increase in the young population. The participation rate by age, however, also increased (see Table 4.4, p. 104). Some of the increased participation may be attributed to the introduction of the free scheme and the free transport service undoubtedly led to increased participation in rural areas.

The rising cost of the school transport system (for first and second level pupils) led the government in 1976 to commission a study of the service. The study was carried out by Hyland Associates Limited, management consultants, and was published in 1979.[15] The report recommended that an annual charge per pupil be levied for use of school buses. The initial reaction of the government, however, was to reject the notion of a levy on the grounds that it would interfere with equality of opportunity.[16] In 1983, amid considerable controversy, a levy was introduced, except for students whose parents qualified for medical cards, i.e. those on low incomes.

Vocational schools
There was little emphasis in Ireland on technical education prior to the early decades of the present century. The Vocational Education Act, 1930, remains the basic statute governing vocational and technical education and has provided the framework for development in this area. The subsequent development of vocational schools helped to redress partially the regional imbalance of secondary schools. The important provisions in the Act covered administration and financial arrangements.

Administration

The Act is administered by local vocational education committees (VECs) subject to the general control of the Minister for Education. Each committee has a minimum of fourteen members selected by the local rating authority and holds office for the same period as the authority. Not more than eight of the members may be members of the rating authority. Membership must be representative of educational, cultural, industrial and commercial interests in the area. There are thirty-eight VECs: one each for the county boroughs (Dublin, Cork, Limerick and Waterford), and seven for certain urban areas (Bray, Drogheda, Dun Laoghaire, Galway, Sligo, Tralee and Wexford), and one for each administrative county.

The functions of a committee are to provide, or assist in the provision of, a system of continuation education and a system of technical education in its area. It may establish schools, employ staff and generally perform all the functions of an education authority, within the general powers conferred by the Act. A committee's programme is subject to the approval of the Minister for Education, but once the basic educational and financial schemes have been approved, a considerable degree of flexibility and discretion is allowed in regard to the actual organisation of courses. Committees are thus in a position to be responsive to local needs.

In May 1974 the Minister for Education, Richard Burke, requested all VECs to establish boards of management in each of their schools by 31 October 1974. By 1990 boards of management had been established in the majority of vocational schools and they normally consist of six VEC members, two parents and a teacher. These boards are sub-committees of the local VEC.

Finance

The financial arrangements of the Vocational Education Act provided for a local rate contribution and corresponding grant from the state. In the first year, 1931-32, the total cost of vocational education was £303,000, of which two-thirds was a contribution from the Department of Education. In time, the local rate contribution declined in importance, particularly following the abolition of rates on private dwellings in 1978. At present, over 90 per cent of the total cost of vocational education is by way of grants from the Department of Education with less than 5 per cent of the contribution coming from local rates.

Secondary versus vocational schools
Apart from administrative and financing differences between secondary and vocational schools, a number of other important differences also existed. From the outset, vocational schools have been inter-denominational and co-educational, whereas secondary schools were mainly denominational and single sex. While vocational schools appear to have a more democratic administrative structure, the church nevertheless, has had some influence on the development of the system. At the time of the passing of the Vocational Education Act, the Catholic hierarchy was given an assurance by the Minister for Education that the vocational system would not impinge upon the field covered by the denominationally controlled secondary schools.[17] It is obvious that the two types of schools were to develop quite separately and that there was to be no overlap between them.

Coolahan has remarked that in the 1960s:

> Vocational schools were frequently in unequal competition with the local secondary schools, each type of school proceeding in splendid isolation from the other.[18]

It is only in recent years, with the introduction of leaving certificate courses in vocational schools, that the social and educational barriers between the two systems have begun to be slowly removed. The vocational system with its emphasis on technical subjects was popularly regarded as a type of educational cul-de-sac where qualifications led to low paid occupations; the secondary schools, on the other hand, with their emphasis on academic subjects were regarded as having higher social status, their qualifications being passports to third level academic education and more remunerative occupations.

Despite recent curricular developments, the divisions still remain and are such as to have evoked this remark from Gemma Hussey, Minister for Education 1982-86, following her visit to a number of different schools in north Kerry in 1984:

> The old snob divisions between vocational and secondary are firmly evident. If I was a dictator they would be all mixed up together.[19]

Comprehensive schools
Apart from inequalities based on social groups, the *Investment in Education* report also indicated that there were inequalities based on geographical location in the participation of children in post-primary education.[20] The reasons for this have already been outlined in the foregoing sections. An attempt to remedy this deficiency was the establishment of comprehensive schools, plans for which were first announced in 1963 by the Minister for Education, Dr Patrick Hillery. In his policy statement, the Minister referred to:

> ... areas where the population is so scattered as to make the establishment of a secondary or a vocational school a most unlikely event. Even if it were at all possible through private enterprise to establish a school of the kind required, its smallness would decree that even the best of its pupils would have little choice of subjects in the minimal programme which it could offer. We have ... reached the point where in these particular regions some new kind of approach is needed in post-primary education.[21]

What the Minister envisaged was the establishment, in areas where post-primary education was inadequate or non-existent, of schools which would be completely financed by the state. The first four comprehensive schools were to be established at Cootehill (County Cavan), Carraroe (County Galway), Shannon (County Clare), and Glenties (County Donegal). Each of these schools was sited in rural areas and was open to all children within a radius of ten miles.

The comprehensive school also represented an attempt to rectify the division of interest between secondary and vocational schools by combining academic and practical subjects in one broad curriculum. In this way pupils would be offered an education structured to their needs, abilities and interests. Unlike some secondary schools, there is no entry test.

Protestant comprehensives
Because of the absence of any Protestant equivalent of the
Catholic religious orders which have reinvested members'
salaries in the establishment and maintenance of their
schools, the cost to Protestants of providing their own
secondary schools has been relatively high. The introduction of the concept of a comprehensive school where
capital and current costs are met fully by the state presented
an opportunity to establish Protestant schools without the
burden of heavy costs. Three Protestant comprehensives
have been established, two in Dublin and one in Cork, but
the intake of pupils in these schools is not exclusively
Protestant.

Management and finance
At present there are two basic management structures, one
for Protestant schools and one for the others. The
Protestant comprehensives have a board comprising three
representatives of the Protestant authority, a VEC representative, and an inspector of the Department of
Education. The boards for the other schools comprise one
bishop's nominee, the chief executive officer of the local
VEC, and an inspector of the Department of Education. It
is proposed to amend the structures of these boards to
allow representation from teachers and parents.

Both capital and current costs of comprehensive schools
are met in full by the Department of Education.

Community schools
Another important finding of the *Investment in Education*
report was that there were gaps in the efficiency of the
educational system in the use of existing educational
resources. In particular, the report referred to duplication
of resources and staff in secondary and vocational schools.
In a statement to the authorities of secondary and vocational schools in 1966, the Minister for Education, George
Colley, indicated that the two rigidly separated, post-
primary systems could no longer be maintained, although
their distinctive character should be retained. He recommended a sharing of accommodation and facilities between
schools.[22] His recommendations, however, had little effect.
In 1970, Patrick Faulkner, Minister for Education,

announced plans for community schools to be created by agreement rather than by legislation. The circular on community schools issued by the Minister indicated that in some areas community schools would result from the amalgamation of existing secondary and vocational schools and in growing suburban areas from the development of a single school rather than the traditional development of separate secondary and vocational schools. The community schools were to be co-educational and non-fee paying with enrolments of 400 up to 1,000.

The community school concept seemed a logical development and would help to eliminate many of the obvious deficiencies in the educational system. An added attraction was that the capital costs would be covered mainly by the state and, in a period of rising costs, this would be an incentive to religious orders to participate in community schools. Another dimension to the community school concept was the involvement of the community. The community schools were to be focal points in the locality, their facilities being made available outside school hours to the community in general.

The announcement of plans for community schools gave rise to a considerable controversy. In the debate which followed, opposition was expressed towards the merging of two distinct educational systems. Much of this was undoubtedly influenced by the higher prestige accorded to secondary schools. Not infrequently, parents and religious orders objected to the amalgamation of traditional secondary schools with the vocational system. Controversy also attended the deeds of trust (the legal base for the schools in the absence of legislation) which were to be signed by the main parties. The teachers' unions had objected to certain clauses in the deeds but subsequently withdrew their objections.

By 1990 there were fifty-two community schools (Table 4.2). One of the main factors accounting for the acceptance of the community school concept was the decline in religious orders. As a result of this decline it was virtually impossible for them to establish new secondary schools as they would have done in the past, and increasingly difficult for them to retain a sufficient presence in the existing secondary schools.

Management and finance
Community schools are normally managed by a ten-person
board comprising three religious nominees, three VEC
nominees, two parent representatives and two teacher
representatives, together with the secretary to the board as
a non-voting member.

Current expenditure in community schools is borne
entirely by the state, as are at least 90 per cent of capital
costs, the remainder being met by the religious orders and
the VEC.

Table 4.2: Number of second level schools, 1976 and 1990

	1976/77	1990/91
Secondary	532	476
Vocational	245	248
Comprehensive	15	16
Community	24	52
Other	–	3
Total	816	795

Source: Department of Education, *Statistical Report*

Rationalisation
A number of developments have occurred in the past few
decades which have, to some extent, lessened the distinction
between the traditional secondary and vocational schools.
Thus, the curriculum in these two types of schools is now
broadly analogous. Similarly, the establishment of community schools has ensured that a single school now exists
in some areas where traditionally secondary and vocational
schools would have been established. Nevertheless, it is
difficult to justify the present system where there are four
different types of schools at second level with different
administrative and financial arrangements. Some rationalisation is required.

In 1985, the Department of Education published a Green
Paper entitled *Partners in Education*. It proposed the
abolition of the vocational education committees and their
replacement by thirteen local education councils (LECs),
with a membership representing teachers, parents, school

management, youth services, training agencies, trade unions and employers. The LECs would be responsible for coordinating all secondary, vocational, comprehensive and community schools in their area, and for the provision, planning and development of second level education. The areas to be covered by the LECs would embrace a number of counties in some cases.

The Green Paper pointed out that developments in the post-primary education system over the previous two decades had led to the creation of a number of different types of schools, all of which were seeking to provide essentially the same education service to the same public. It commented that:

> In the context of the rationalisation of school facilities in particular this situation has given rise to controversy between school authorities at post-primary level, a controversy related to issues of school management rather than to educational considerations.[23]

The Green Paper indicated that the establishment of a regional body would eliminate friction based on the management structure of schools and would provide a better framework for the rationalisation of post-primary facilities and for the delivery of other services.

The reaction to the Green Paper by the various interest groups was not very enthusiastic. Thus, the abolition of the vocational education committees was unacceptable to many members of those committees, especially public elected representatives. Similarly, the reaction of the teachers' unions in second level schools was muted although the Irish National Teachers' Organisation, representing teachers in primary schools, objected to the plan on the grounds that primary schools were not included in the proposed regionalised structure.

While the rationalisation as envisaged by the Green Paper is unlikely to come about in the near future, a certain rationalisation at second level would now appear to be inevitable. This arises mainly from the decline in religious orders and schools under their control. The present situation in many towns of a secondary school for girls run by a religious order, a secondary school for boys run by a religious order, and a co-educational vocational school is likely to change as the religious orders' involvement in education declines further. This will inevitably lead to a rationalisation of the system at local level.

Third level education
Third level education in Ireland may be broadly divided into two sectors, i.e. university and non-university.

Non-university sector
The regional technical colleges (RTCs), the colleges of the Dublin Institute of Technology (DIT), the teacher training colleges and a number of other institutions providing courses in areas such as domestic science, commerce, retail distribution and management studies, provide most further education in Ireland outside universities. It is a sector which has grown considerably in the past two decades.

Regional technical colleges
The idea of the regional technical colleges was first mentioned in a policy statement on post-primary education in 1963 by the Minister for Education, Dr Patrick Hillery.[24] It was his intention to arrange for the provision of, amongst others, a limited number of technological colleges with regional status. The colleges were to work towards a projected technical leaving certificate. The idea was taken further in 1969 by a steering committee on technical education set up in 1966 by Donogh O'Malley, Minister for Education. This steering committee still saw the colleges as, for the most part, second level institutions but suggested that some of them might also provide post-leaving certificate full-time or equivalent part-time courses over one or two years leading to higher technician courses.[25] Both the report of the steering committee on technical education and the *Investment in Education* report stressed the need in Ireland for high level technicians to service a growing industrial sector.

The first regional technical colleges opened in the period 1970-72 at Athlone, Carlow, Dundalk, Galway, Sligo, Letterkenny and Waterford. While they were originally intended to reinforce the technical dimension of the second level system, they quickly found themselves called upon to cater increasingly for third level demand. All of the courses in the RTCs are now third level and encompass degree, certificate and diploma courses.

Under the Regional Technical Colleges Act of 1992 the RTCs were given greater autonomy from the VECs under which they operated. The Act established them as self-governing institutions with a governing body representative of the local vocational education committee, staff, students and other relevant organisations. All finance (capital and current) for RTCs is provided by the Department of Education. Under the Act the former Limerick College of Art, Commerce and Technology (CoACT) has become the Limerick RTC, while the Cork School of Music and Crawford College of Art and Design have become part of the existing Cork RTC.

Dublin Institute of Technology

The Dublin Institute of Technology (DIT), formerly a sub-committee of the City of Dublin VEC, comprises six colleges, i.e. technology (2), catering, commerce, marketing and design, and music. The 1992 Dublin Institute of Technology Act provided for greater autonomy for the DIT and its own governing body. Professional level courses in the DIT are eligible for degrees awarded by University of Dublin (Trinity College).

Colleges of education

There are four colleges of education for primary school teachers: St Patrick's, Drumcondra; Church of Ireland College; St Mary's, Marino, all in Dublin; and Mary Immaculate College in Limerick. Carysfort Teacher Training College, established in 1883, was closed in 1988. There are two colleges for home economics (St Catherine's in Dublin, and St Angela's in Sligo). Teachers of art are trained in the National College of Art and Design, Dublin, which is associated for degree purposes with the National Council for Educational Awards. The colleges of education and the two colleges of home economics are associated with the universities for their degree awards.

Until recently, two other institutions, the National Institutes for Higher Education at Limerick and Dublin, were part of the non-university sector. In 1989, however, these became the University of Limerick and Dublin City University, respectively.

National Council for Educational Awards
Following proposals made to the Minister for Education by the steering committee on technical education in 1969 and the recommendations of the Higher Education Authority (HEA) in 1969, the National Council for Educational Awards (NCEA) was set up by the government in April 1972 on an *ad hoc* basis pending the passing of legislation to establish it on a statutory basis. Following a period of uncertainty concerning its future in the mid-1970s, the NCEA Act was passed in 1978 and came into effect in July 1980. The NCEA is responsible for the coordination, development, and promotion of technical, industrial, scientific, technological and commercial education, and education in art and design outside the universities. It fulfils this role by the approval of courses and the granting and conferring of degrees, diplomas, certificates and other educational awards. The NCEA does not, however, award all the degrees outside universities since, as already pointed out, some third level institutions, e.g. the Dublin Institute of Technology and the colleges of education, have associated themselves either with the National University of Ireland or University of Dublin (Trinity College) for degree awards.

University sector
There are now four universities in the Republic: Dublin University with one college, Trinity College (TCD); the National University of Ireland (NUI) with three constituent colleges at Dublin (UCD), Cork (UCC), and Galway (UCG); Dublin City University; and University of Limerick.
   St Patrick's College, Maynooth, the national Catholic seminary, is recognised by the National University of Ireland for degree awarding purposes. There is also an independent medical school, the Royal College of Surgeons in Ireland, founded in 1784.

Trinity College
Dublin University received its charter from Elizabeth I in 1591. From the beginning it was identified with English rule and the governing class in Ireland. For much of its

history, according to F.S.L. Lyons, Trinity was 'intensely conscious of its position as a bastion of the Ascendancy in general and of Anglicanism in particular'.[26] In 1793 Catholics were admitted to degrees in Trinity College and by the mid-nineteenth century they constituted about 10 per cent of the undergraduate body.

The Queen's Colleges, 1845

In 1845 Sir Robert Peel introduced a Bill providing for the establishment of three 'Queen's Colleges' in Ireland. The colleges were to be established at Belfast, Galway and Cork. There would be no interference with religious convictions, but the establishment, by private endowment, of a theological school within the colleges was permissible. Opposition to the Bill was considerable, particularly from some members of the Irish Catholic hierarchy who feared that lectures in philosophy, history and science were bound to reflect contemporary thought on these subjects. At the Synod of Thurles (1850) the hierarchy condemned the Queen's Colleges and exhorted laymen to avoid them as students or teachers on the grounds that they were dangers to faith and morals. A minority of bishops unsuccessfully appealed against these decisions. Despite ecclesiastical opposition, the three colleges were established.

The Royal University, 1879

The University Education (Ireland) Act, 1879, provided for the formation of a new university (the Royal University) and for the dissolution of the Queen's University. The Royal University was modelled on the University of London, which at the time was purely an examining body. Authority was granted to confer degrees on all students irrespective of where they had studied. The religious difficulty was overcome and Catholics and Protestants presented themselves for examination.

The Catholic University, 1854

At the Synod of Thurles a section of the Catholic hierarchy favoured the establishment of a Catholic university styled on that of Louvain, which had been founded with papal approval in 1834. Dr John Henry Newman, a distinguished Oxford convert to Catholicism, was invited to become rector of the new university. An application by the hierarchy for a charter for the university was unsuccessful, as was an application for state funds. Newman left Ireland in 1858 and the university declined. In 1890 it was placed in the charge of the Jesuits who administered its affairs until the establishment of the National University in 1908.

The National University of Ireland, 1908
The National University of Ireland was established by the Irish Universities Act, 1908. In the following year the Royal University was formally dissolved. The Act provided for the establishment of two new universities, one in Dublin and one in Belfast. The one in Belfast was to become the Queen's University, replacing the former college of that name. The new National University of Ireland, centred in Dublin, was to take over the Queen's Colleges in Cork and Galway as constituent colleges as well as the new college founded in Dublin to replace the Catholic University. It was further allowed to affiliate 'such institutions as have a standard deemed satisfactory by the University', an arrangement which allowed the subsequent entry of Maynooth. No test whatever of religious belief was to be permitted for any appointment in either of the universities, thus denying the denominational university which the Catholic hierarchy had long demanded.

St Patrick's College, Maynooth
St Patrick's was founded in 1795 as a seminary for the training of the Catholic clergy. It was the only Catholic educational institution to receive state aid at the time. In 1910, under the provisions of the Irish Universities Act, 1908, the College was recognised by the Senate of the National University as a recognised college of the University in certain faculties. A decision by the hierarchy to admit lay students to courses at Maynooth in 1966-67 led to the wider use of an institution which had hitherto been confined to the training of priests. Since then the number of clerical students has declined while the number of lay students has increased steadily.

Trinity College in the twentieth century
The future status of Trinity College became a leading

question during the early years of the present century. A Royal Commission of 1907 recommended that Dublin University should be enlarged to include the Queen's Colleges, and that a new college acceptable to the Catholic authorities be founded in Dublin. Opposition to this proposal, however, ensured that Trinity maintained its independence when the National University was established in 1908.

At the National Synod of Maynooth in 1875, the Catholic hierarchy had coupled Trinity College with the Queen's Colleges as places forbidden to Catholic students. Yet for many years the bishops took no active steps towards implementing this decision, apart from periodical instructions to priests to refrain from advising parents to send their children to Trinity College. After 1944, the archbishop of Dublin began issuing annual condemnations of the attendance of Catholics at Trinity in his lenten pastorals. Such attendance would, he affirmed, be permissible only for 'grave and valid reasons'. The consequence was not only to limit the entry of Catholic students, but that of students from the lower income groups as well. Local authorities proved unwilling to oppose the hierarchy's position by offering scholarships under the 1908 Act to Trinity College, though some were prepared to award them in special circumstances to Protestant candidates alone. The most commonly accepted 'grave and valid reason' was an inability to take the compulsory matriculation qualification in Irish which was required by the National University. Perhaps the most significant barriers created by the ban were not so much religious as social and it served to isolate Trinity from the life of the vast majority of the Irish people.

The regulations of the Catholic hierarchy in regard to the attendance of Catholics at Trinity College were outlined in the report of the Commission on Higher Education.[27] In the report, Bishop Philbin referred to the colleges of the National University as substantially satisfying Catholic requirements, whereas Trinity College was seen as having a neutral and secularist character.[28]

One effect of the ban was to lead to an influx of non-Irish undergraduates. In 1965-66, 27 per cent of Trinity's students were from the United Kingdom (excluding Northern Ireland), and a further 9 per cent were from other foreign countries. In the same year Catholics accounted for 20 per cent of the total number of students. In 1967 the Board of Trinity College decided to limit the entry of non-Irish students, up to a maximum of 10 per cent, to those who had associations with Ireland or those who belonged to educationally-developing countries. This measure partly paved the way for the removal of the ban which occurred in 1970. By 1975-76, 3 per cent of Trinity's students were from the United Kingdom (excluding Northern Ireland), and 6 per cent were from other foreign countries. In the same year Catholics accounted for 65 per cent of students at the college.

University of Limerick and Dublin City University
Reference has already been made to the former National Institutes for Higher Education at Limerick and Dublin which were granted university status in 1989. The idea of an Institute in Limerick was first put forward by the Higher Education Authority in 1969. The Institute began functioning in 1972 offering degree and diploma courses with a strong bias towards technology and European studies. The National Institute for Higher Education in Dublin was established in 1975; the first students were enrolled in 1980.

Higher Education Authority
The Higher Education Authority was established in 1968 on the recommendation of the Commission on Higher Education but it was not until 1972 that it became a statutory body following the passing of the Higher Education Authority Act, 1971. The HEA has two main functions:

• As an advisory body it must monitor, review, advise and play its part generally in furthering the development of higher education and in the coordination of state investment therein.
• Its central statutory power and function as an executive body is to assess in relation to annual or other periods the financial requirements of the institutions of which it is the funding agency; to recommend for state grants the capital and current amounts so assessed and to allocate to the institutions concerned the state funds provided.

Finance for third level

The two main sources of recurrent funds for third level institutions are state grants, the most significant source, and students' fees. As a proportion of income, students' fees fell from about 20 per cent in the late 1960s to below 15 per cent a decade later. They have increased since then and by 1988-89 they accounted for 30 per cent of total income in the university colleges and 31 per cent in the other institutions funded by the Higher Education Authority. In this context the Authority noted its concern about the possible implications of further increases in real terms in fees for equality of opportunity of access to and demand for university education.[29]

Enrolment at third level

The introduction of free post-primary education, the availability of higher education grants, the expansion of the non-university sector, as well as the burgeoning youth population, have inevitably meant an increase in the numbers attending third level institutions since the mid-1960s. The largest increase has been in the non-university sector outside of the colleges of education. This is largely due to the establishment of regional technical colleges and the NIHEs at Limerick and Dublin.

In the mid-1960s universities accounted for over four-fifths (82 per cent) of full-time students in third level institutions, but by 1988-89 this had declined to just under three-fifths (67 per cent). The number of places in private institutions which are not state aided has also grown.

Higher education grants

The report of the Commission on Higher Education contained surveys carried out by an Investment in Education team and by Monica Nevin which indicated that children of manual workers comprised less than one-tenth of university students, farmers' children not more than two-tenths, with the children of non-manual workers accounting for the remainder.[30] Consequently, the Commission felt that while scholarships would assist students of limited means but with special abilities, and loans would remove immediate barriers to higher education for the qualified student, there was need for additional assistance available only to students from the lower income groups. This assistance, the Commission envisaged, would take the form of a grant and would further remove financial barriers, and by providing a special incentive might also help to remove psychological barriers. The Local Authority (Higher Education Grant) Act, 1968, provided for such a scheme, with grants available to students who reach a required standard in the leaving certificate examination and whose parents satisfy a means test. The grant is administered by local authorities and is operated on a sliding scale related to parental income and number of children in the family. It also distinguishes between students living within commuting distances of third level centres and others.

Another type of funding for higher education is that provided by the European Social Fund (ESF) Training Grants Scheme introduced in 1986. This scheme covers one-year and two-year programmes at national certificate level in the RTCs and in the colleges of technology. These ESF grants cover course fees and in 1992 a means test was introduced for the maintenance element which is related to proximity of the family residence to the third level college.

In 1986, 21.8 per cent of student new-entrants to third level institutions were in receipt of a higher education grant and 39.4 per cent were in receipt of an ESF grant. In the same year, over one-third (37.3 per cent) of all new entrants to third level institutions were not in receipt of any public financial aid.[31]

Rationalisation at third level
For almost a quarter of a century now, there has been debate and controversy surrounding the status of different third level institutions. Between 1967 and 1977 a variety of proposals and counter-proposals were put forward, either by the Minister for Education or others, such as the report of the Commission on Higher Education and the Higher Education Authority (HEA). Essentially these proposals were concerned with the number of universities and with which colleges should have university status. The classic example of the bewildering changes and proposals were those made by Richard Burke, Minister for Education, 1973-76. In 1974 he indicated that Trinity College would

retain its status as a separate university, University College Dublin would become an independent university, and the NUI would remain (with constituent colleges in Cork and Galway), i.e. there would be three universities. In July 1976, however, in a complete turnabout in policy, he announced that there were to be five universities (Trinity, UCD, UCC, UCG, and Maynooth). Neither of these proposals has so far been implemented.

As a result of a national referendum on the seventh amendment to the Constitution held in July 1979, it is now possible for the government to introduce legislation providing for the abolition of the NUI and the establishment of independent universities at UCD, UCC and UCG. However, no concrete proposals have been put forward to this effect.

Tussing has argued that 'one of the major anomalies in the Irish system of education is the organisation of third level education'. He pointed out that the third level institutions can be categorised or classified in different ways, e.g. by means of funding, by degree-awarding status, or by curriculum specialisation, but that the categorisation yields wholly different groupings.[32]

There is little doubt that the present situation at third level in relation to funding and general structures remains somewhat confused. Thus, for example, the Higher Education Authority is responsible for funding institutions which are designated under the Higher Education Authority Act, yet there is no rationale as to why some third level institutions have not yet been so designated. The National Council for Educational Awards, on the other hand, is responsible for the coordination, development and promotion of various forms of education in third level institutions outside universities. Yet it seems ironic that some of these institutions have chosen, for whatever reason, to associate themselves with universities for degree purposes rather than with the NCEA. The Higher Education Authority would appear to have an advisory role in relation to third level education in general, yet it must be difficult for the Authority to fulfil this function because of the existing funding arrangements under which certain third level institutions need have no reference whatsoever to the Higher Education Authority. The HEA has commented that this situation has resulted in a sectional approach to the consideration of higher education.[33]

Adult education

With the introduction of important developments in the Irish educational system at all levels during the 1960s and early 1970s, it was inevitable that attention would be focused on adult education and, more specifically, on those who, for whatever reason, had terminated their full-time education at an early age.

In 1973 a report on adult education in Ireland was published.[34] The report was instigated by the Minister for Education in 1969 and he established a committee to 'carry out a survey of the needs of the community in the matter of adult education and to indicate the type of permanent organisation to be set up in order to serve those needs'. The report estimated that 10 per cent of the adult population participated annually in adult education, considered that the expenditure on adult education was inadequate to meet even existing needs and recommended that separate budgetary provision be made in the Department of Education for adult education. Among its main structural recommendations was the establishment of county education committees.

In 1984 yet another report on adult education, *Lifelong Learning*, was published. This report had also been instigated by the Minister for Education who established a Commission in 1981, with wide terms of reference, to prepare a national development plan for adult and continuing education. The Commission defined adult education to include:

> ... all systematic learning by adults which contributes to their development as individuals and as members of the community and of society apart from full-time instruction received by persons as part of their uninterrupted initial education and training. It may be formal education, which takes place in institutions, e.g. training centres, schools, colleges, institutes and universities; or non-formal education, which is any other systematic form of learning, including self-directed learning.[35]

As part of its task the Commission carried out a survey of attitudes towards, and participation in, adult education.

This survey indicated that the group which had not participated in any form of education since completing initial education had within it disproportionately high numbers of older and working class people and rural dwellers, i.e. those who have in general benefitted least from initial education compared with their younger, middle class and urban counterparts. The Commission recommended that local adult education boards be set up under the VECs with a separate budget to enable priorities to be established on a local basis. It also recommended the establishment of a national education council. Among the developments which have occurred were the appointment of adult education organisers in 1979 under the VECs and the establishment of adult education boards in each VEC area in 1984. These boards are responsible for assessing the educational needs in their area and preparing suitable programmes.

Adult education courses are mainly provided by statutory agencies, notably the VECs. Many other organisations and institutions, both statutory and voluntary, are involved in adult education. These provide a variety of courses from basic literacy to leisure-type courses.

Aontas is the national umbrella organisation representing adult education both statutory and voluntary. In its report, *For Adults Only* (1989), Aontas provides an overview of the issues and problems facing the development of adult education. It points out that:

> Adult education in Ireland is underdeveloped ... Another problem facing adult education is that it is more oriented in range and practice towards the middle classes following hobby and leisure pursuits than as a direct means towards improving their life chances. Often those who have most to benefit tend to be excluded.[36]

Aontas recommended that a clear and definite administrative structure regarding all aspects of adult education should be established and that every pertinent method should be tried to increase the participation of disadvantaged groups and individuals.

Participation in education
The schoolgoing population has grown considerably since

the mid-1960s as a result of the increase in the birthrate. This increase in population has been particularly reflected in the growth in numbers of pupils enrolled at first level. The composition of the schoolgoing population has undergone some change over the past two decades (Table 4.3). Pupils at first level now account for a smaller proportion of total schoolgoing population than they did in the mid-1960s. Similarly the percentage share at third level has increased over that time. With the fall in the birthrate it is now expected that the schoolgoing population will decline and this will be reflected initially at first level.

While there has been a general increase in the numbers attending second and third level, it is more relevant to examine trends in participation rates. Since the mid-1960s, prior to the introduction of free post-primary education, the participation rates for those aged fifteen to nineteen years had increased remarkably by 1990 (Table 4.4).

Table 4.3: Full-time students in education, 1965-1990

	1965-66		1975-76		1990-91	
	Number	%	Number	%	Number	%
First level	504,900	75.5	550,100	64.4	552,528	57.1
Second level	142,900	21.4	271,000	31.7	345,941	35.7
Third level	20,700	3.1	33,100	3.9	69,988	7.2
Total	668,500	100.0	854,200	100.0	968,457	100.0

Source: Department of Education, *Statistical Report*

Table 4.4: Participation rate in full-time education by age, 1966-1990

Age	1966	1974	1990
15 years	54.2	77.5	99.0
16 years	39.0	60.4	92.5
17 years	27.3	43.1	74.2
18 years	14.7	22.4	47.6
19 years	9.6	12.5	31.0

Source: Department of Education, *Statistical Report*

Participation at third level

At third level, serious disparities exist in relation to participation by students from different social classes. A survey of entrants to third level education from the Dublin area in 1978-79 indicated that about three-quarters of entrants came from the four higher socio-economic groups, despite the fact that these groups constituted only one-fifth of the population of Dublin.[37] The study also revealed distinct geographic differences within Dublin, reflecting the socio-economic composition of the population in different areas.

In 1982, a report on the national situation by Clancy revealed an uneven geographical and social group distribution of entrants to third level institutions throughout the country.[38] The report indicated that a considerably higher proportion of young people from counties in the west of Ireland go on to third level education: the lowest level of participation is in a band of midland counties while Dublin, Wexford and Wicklow also have low participation rates. Geographic proximity to a third level college is a significant factor which helps to explain high rates in Galway, Cork, Carlow, but there are also high rates in counties without a third level centre and Dublin, with a number of third level centres, is one of the most 'depressed' areas.

The report also confirmed previous findings concerning participation by socio-economic group. Thus, participation by students from professional and managerial groups was disproportionately high. Students from fee-paying secondary schools are the most likely to go on to third level, free secondary schools are next, followed by comprehensive and community schools, with vocational school students the least likely.

In 1988, yet another report by Clancy, *Who Goes to College?*, updated and provided a comparison with the findings of the 1982 report.[39] In terms of participation by social group the position remained basically similar to that of 1982. The exception was increased participation of farmers' children to a position where they were over-represented in relation to their numbers in the general population (Table 4.5). Participation rates by county were higher than in 1980 – all but one, Donegal, showing a noticeable increase. Rates for the western counties remained high and the lowest were

Table 4.5: Participation ratio by socio-economic status of entrants to higher education, 1980 and 1986

Socio-economic group	Participation ratio* 1980	1986
Farmers	1.04	1.45
Other agricultural occupations	0.21	0.48
Higher professionals	3.93	3.00
Lower professionals	2.29	2.14
Employers & managers	2.75	1.72
Salaried employees	2.93	2.30
Intermediate non-manual workers	1.11	1.21
Other non-manual workers	0.50	0.45
Skilled manual workers	0.51	0.51
Semi-skilled manual workers	0.49	0.42
Unskilled manual workers	0.11	0.16

*The participation ratio is calculated by relating the number of entrants to higher education by socio-economic group to the population under fifteen years in that group in 1981.

Source: P. Clancy, *Who Goes to College?* (1988), Table 7, p. 22

Donegal, Offaly, Dublin, although the participation rate in Donegal is improved when the numbers who enrolled in Northern Ireland colleges from that county is taken into account (Table 4.6).

Equality of opportunity
It can be argued that the issue of equality of access to all levels of education is not unrelated to public expenditure at different levels. There is little correlation between the share of current expenditure and the share of students at each level. Thus, third level accounts for just over 7 per cent of all full-time students but one-fifth of current expenditure (Table 4.7). There are reasons for the unit costs being higher at second level and third level as compared with first level but it is the scale of the difference which has been questioned. For some time it has been apparent that the per capita expenditure at first level, i.e. during the years of compulsory schooling, is much less than that at second level and significantly less than that at third level. While the differential has narrowed somewhat over the past decade or so (Table 4.8) the fact remains that in 1991 expenditure for

Table 4.6: Rates of admission to higher education by county of permanent residence, 1980 and 1986

| County | Admission rate* | |
	1980	1986
Carlow	29	32
Dublin	17	20
Kildare	16	24
Kilkenny	20	27
Laois	15	23
Longford	21	30
Louth	23	25
Meath	16	25
Offaly	15	20
Westmeath	20	31
Wexford	18	22
Wicklow	18	23
Clare	20	30
Cork	22	28
Kerry	25	35
Limerick	20	27
Tipperary	19	27
Waterford	23	28
Galway	28	33
Leitrim	19	34
Mayo	23	31
Roscommon	20	28
Sligo	25	35
Cavan	16	24
Donegal	21	19
Monaghan	20	24
Average	20	25

* The rates of admission are calculated by relating the actual number of admissions to the average of the populations of the single years of age from which more than 75 per cent of the new entrants came.

Source: P. Clancy, *Who Goes to College?* (1988), Table 21, p. 47

third level students was at three and a half times that per first level students.

In this context the *Report of the Primary Education Review Body* highlighted the fact that the per capita grant in primary schools (£28 plus local contribution of £7) was considerably less than that in secondary schools (£150) which in itself is regarded as inadequate, leading many

Table 4.7: Current expenditure on education* by level, 1990

	£m	%
First level	495,033	38.6
Second level	524,063	40.9
Third level	262,461	20.5
Total	1,281,557	100.0

* Excludes £4.9 million on special schools.

Source: Department of Education, *Statistical Report*

Table 4.8: Public expenditure (per capita) at first, second and third level education, 1980 and 1991

	1980		1991	
	£	Ratio	£	Ratio
First level	339	(1.00)	950	(1.00)
Second level	651	(1.92)	1,550	(1.63)
Third level	1,694	(4.99)	3,425	(3.60)

Source: National Planning Board, *Proposal for Plan 1984-1987* (Dublin, Stationery Office, 1984), p. 291; *Dáil Debates*, 20 March 1991

secondary schools to seek a voluntary contribution from parents. The Review Body refers to a survey carried out by the National Parents' Council (Primary) which indicated that nationally, 59 per cent of school funds came from the capitation grant, 6 per cent from other Department of Education grants, with 35 per cent being contributed by the parents either directly or through the parish contribution.[40]

Not only do those who go on to third level receive the highest subsidies but they are also more likely to be from the higher socio-economic groups and are more likely to obtain more remunerative employment than those who have completed their education at first or second level. Not surprisingly, therefore, higher expenditure at first level has been recommended as a means of ensuring greater equality of opportunity in education.

Tussing has argued that reasonable equality of opportunity, insofar as it involves schooling and school expenditure, requires concentration on first level.[41] He maintained that the consequences of inadequate schooling at that level probably cannot be rectified and certainly cannot be rectified at any reasonable cost later on. From the mid-1980s, various methods to improve the situation in primary schools in disadvantaged areas were introduced, such as improved pupil-teacher ratio and additional funding. Schools qualifying are in areas of high unemployment and are generally concentrated in large urban areas. The *Programme for Economic and Social Progress* (PESP) made the following commitment:

> Particular attention must be paid to children suffering educational or social disadvantage through early identification of those children allied to positive intervention to support them through the provision of remedial teaching, guidance and counselling and the development of home/ school links. Such a programme will in itself increase retention rates in education among disadvantaged groups.[42]

The PESP also aimed to reduce the overall pupil-teacher ratio to 25:1, a process which will meet the needs of the disadvantaged.

It must be recognised that there are probably limits to which educational policy measures alone can bring about real equality of opportunity. Thus, for example, the provision of additional facilities and supports in disadvantaged areas may not be sufficient in themselves to counteract the influence of other serious social problems in the home environment such as low income, high unemployment and poor housing, which impinge on educational development.

Education policy
Reference has been made at the beginning of this chapter to the lack of a comprehensive legislative base for the education system. This in itself has, at times, hindered the development of educational policy.

Seán O'Connor, former Secretary of the Department of Education, has pointed out that it is only since the early 1960s that the Minister for Education and the Department of Education began to take a lead role in policy formation. Up to then the Department seemed content to leave the control of the system to the three main interest groups, the church, teachers' unions and parents. O'Connor indicates that of these groups the church exerted the most decisive influence; the teachers' unions were mainly concerned with working conditions and remuneration, and parents only became involved to protest at inadequate facilities in their local school.[43]

Even when the Department of Education or the Minister assumed a lead role in policy making, difficulties could still arise in obtaining agreement among the various interests. The problems associated with the establishment of management boards in primary schools in the mid-1970s exemplifies the difficulties of effecting change by agreement. Similar problems arose in relation to community schools.

Much of the analysis which influenced developments until recently was contained in reports of independent review bodies, e.g. the *Investment in Education* report carried out by the Organisation for Economic Cooperation and Development. Policy documents emanating from the Department of Education itself have been few enough in number until recent years. The White Paper on *Educational Development* (1980), which had been promised since 1973, had been expected to deal with a range of fundamental issues in the education system. The general reaction to the White Paper however was one of disappointment in educational and general circles. The following extract from an editorial in the *Irish Press* on the day following the publication of the White Paper (19 December 1980) summarises the popular criticism:

> The White Paper ... is open to serious criticism for what it does not contain. There is no timescale or costing on the proposals and insufficient government commitment to their implementation.

Professor A.D. Tussing, whose report, *Irish Educational Expenditures – Past, Present and Future* (1978), had given rise to considerable debate arising from his controversial suggestions regarding modifying the free post-primary education scheme, was highly critical of the White Paper for the issues it failed to address. His sardonic summary of the White Paper was as follows:

The educational system in this country is essentially a good one and is not in need of alteration. The period of change is ended. Enrolment growth is slowing. There is no public pressure for innovation. The issues most discussed by educators and the community are not worthy of mention. And the money is not there for new departures anyway.[44]

Tussing went on to recount the issues which he felt should have been addressed in the White Paper, i.e. the lack of accountability and adequate planning in the system, the relative priorities in the allocation of funds at each level and the extent to which the structure of education reinforces divisions among students (denominational, sex, social class).

In contrast to the White Paper, the reaction to the *Programme for Action in Education, 1984-1987,* published by the Department of Education following submissions from different interest groups, was more favourable. It spelled out a whole series of issues which the government intended to tackle and at the same time left scope for further discussion and consultation.

The present situation is open to the criticism that in the absence of a legal framework decisions regarding the education system can be made without reference to the Oireachtas. The Minister for Education, therefore, may issue circulars and regulations as administrative measures but lacking statutory power. There are few pieces of legislation dealing with first and second level while at third level a number of institutions and organisations have been established by legislation.

In November 1990 the Minister for Education, Mary O'Rourke, announced her intention to issue a White Paper to be followed by public discussion and an Education Act. The PESP (1991) reiterated these views but added that a Green Paper, comprehensive in its coverage, would be published in 1991 affording the opportunity to all parties to offer views prior to the publication of a White Paper in 1992 and the introduction of an Education Act.[45]

Green Paper 1992
Following two changes of ministers, leaks of drafts to the media, and the highly unusual step of publishing an

introduction to the Green Paper in April to coincide with the annual conference of the teachers' unions, the Green Paper, *Education for a Changing World*, was finally published in June 1992 by the Minister for Education, Seamus Brennan. Apparently the published version has undergone some changes from the proposals of Mary O'Rourke. The Green Paper identified six key aims for the development of education into the next century:

• to establish greater equity in education – particularly for those who are disadvantaged socially, economically, physically and mentally
• to broaden Irish education, so as to equip students more effectively for life, for work in an enterprise culture, and for citizenship of Europe
• to make the best use of education resources, by radically devolving administration, introducing the best management practice and strengthening policy making
• to train and develop teachers so as to equip them for a constantly changing environment
• to create a system of effective quality assurance
• to ensure greater openness and accountability throughout the system, and to maximise parent involvement and choice.

The following were among the main proposals:

• raising of the school leaving age from fifteen to sixteen years
• all primary and second level schools (including vocational schools) to have a board of management representative of owners or trustees, parents, teachers, school principal and the local business community
• devolution of power from the Department of Education to school boards which would have to produce a school plan, issue an annual report on all aspects of its work and report to parents and the community on its performance and achievements
• maximising the number of primary schools of four teachers or more in rural areas and eight teachers or more in urban areas
• state aided secondary schools to have an admission

policy that will not discriminate on the basis of means, educational level or social background.

Among the initial criticisms of the Green Paper by teachers' unions were the aspirational nature of many proposals and the lack of commitment to additional funding. The Green Paper did not address many key issues on education, such as rationalisation of structures at second level (as proposed in the Green Paper of 1985) or the method and level of funding schools. Otherwise, as a discussion document it has provided a comprehensive basis for a White Paper and, ultimately, an Education Act.

5

Health Services

Introduction

Over several decades the state has assumed greater responsibility for the provision and funding of health services. Barrington, in an excellent account of the interplay of factors influencing the development of Irish health services, has stated:

> In 1900, governmental responsibility for the health of the population was limited to controlling outbreaks of the most serious epidemic diseases and ensuring access by the poor to general practitioner services and Poor Law infirmaries. By 1970, government had accepted responsibility for providing a high standard of medical care for all sections of the population at no or at a heavily subsidised cost to the recipient.[1]

Increased state involvement in the provision of health services did not occur without some opposition from the Catholic Church and the medical profession. The classic instance of this was the Mother and Child Scheme which Dr Noel Browne, Minister for Health (1948-51), proposed to introduce. The Catholic hierarchy opposed the scheme (which would have provided free health service for women before, during and after childbirth and for children up to sixteen years) on the grounds that it represented undue state intervention. The medical profession opposed the scheme because it did not want a comprehensive state health service, preferring instead a mix of public and private.[2]

The change from a locally controlled and largely locally funded system to an increasingly centralised and centrally financed one is another feature of the development of the health services during this century.

More difficult to determine with precision, however, is the extent to which increased public expenditure on health care has led to improved health status in the community. There are, however, some obvious health indicators which have shown dramatic improvement. Thus, for example, life expectancy has increased, infant mortality has been reduced, as has the incidence of infectious diseases, such as tuberculosis. It should be noted, however, that many factors may affect the level of health of the community, e.g. improved living standards in general. It is therefore at least arguable that health standards may well have improved even in the absence of public health programmes.

In recent years two trends are discernible. Firstly, there is the concern, not alone in Ireland, with the escalating cost of public health care. This has given rise to public expenditure cutbacks and attempts to seek more cost-effective services. Secondly, there has been a general tendency to emphasise the importance of health promotion, i.e. the promotion of positive health rather than the traditional emphasis on curing illness. The Health Education Bureau in a report *Promoting Health Through Public Policy* (1987), indicated that much of the premature mortality (e.g. due to heart disease and cancer) and illness is associated with lifestyle (e.g. smoking, diet) and the general environment and is therefore preventable. The Department of Health in its document *Health: The Wider Dimensions* (1986), points out that up to now the focus of health policy has been too narrow, whereas in fact health is a multi-faceted problem and is linked to a greater or lesser degree to all aspects of life. It therefore recommended a more broadly based approach to health policy.

Administration
Hensey[3] has already outlined in admirable detail the evolution of the administrative structure for health care in Ireland and, consequently, only the major developments are reviewed here. State health services were first provided in a rudimentary form under the Poor Law (Ireland) Act, 1838. The Poor Law administration provided infirmaries and other forms of medical care in association with the

workhouses established in each Poor Law union. Unions were administrative units and the total number covering the present area of the Republic was 126. In 1851, the unions were further divided into dispensary districts, to each of which a physician was attached whose duty it was to attend, without charge, to the sick poor of the area. This dispensary system survived up to 1972.

In 1872 the Irish Poor Law Commissioners were abolished and replaced by the Local Government Board for Ireland which assumed control of both Poor Law and health services. Central control became more pronounced following independence when, in 1924, the Department of Local Government and Public Health was established. In 1947 this Department was divided into three – Local Government, Health and Social Welfare.

At local level the administrative structure for health services remained highly complex throughout the nineteenth century and well into the present century. There were a number of agencies with responsibility for various aspects of health care; boards of guardians, for example, which had been established in each Poor Law union continued in existence until 1923. By 1940 most health functions at local level had been transferred to county councils and the county manager became responsible for the formulation of local policy on health services. The transfer of responsibility for all health services to local authorities was completed in 1947 when they assumed responsibility in urban areas for preventive health services which up to then had been the domain of urban district councils. In 1947 there were thirty-one health authorities in the state corresponding to the same number of county councils and county boroughs. In 1960, however, this number was reduced to twenty-seven when unified health authorities were established within the four counties containing the main cities of Dublin, Cork, Limerick and Waterford; the health functions of Dublin County Council and Dublin County Borough, for example, were amalgamated. The trend towards a reduction in the number of authorities with responsibility for health services was taken a stage further when the 1970 Health Act provided for the establishment of eight regional boards.

The reasons for the regionalisation of health functions

were outlined in a White Paper in 1966.[4] They were based
mainly on the following considerations:

- The state had taken over the major share of the costs of
  running the services which were increasing substantially
  every year. It was therefore desirable to have a new
  administrative framework to combine national and local
  interests.

- It was becoming more and more obvious that in order to
  develop the medical service itself, especially in relation
  to acute hospital care, it would be necessary to have the
  organisation on an inter-county basis. It was clear that
  the county as a unit was unsuitable; it was too small as an
  area for hospital services.

- The removal of health affairs from the general local
  authority sphere had been foreshadowed as far back as
  1947 when the Department of Health was separated from
  the Department of Local Government and set up as a
  separate ministry.

Under the provisions of the Health Act, 1970, the
administrative structure of the health services was changed
as from 1 April 1970. From that date the health services
were to be administered by eight health boards, each
covering a number of counties (see Table 5.1).

In setting up the boards, consideration was given to the
area, size of population, and the regions delimited for local
government planning and development. As can be seen
from Table 5.1, however, the populations of the regions
vary with, for example, the Eastern Health Board area
having a population approximately six times that of the
Midland or North Western Health Board areas. Some of
these differences, however, are explained by the density of
population and the location of existing facilities, especially
hospitals.

The membership of each health board varies from
twenty-seven to thirty-five and is a combination of three
main interests:

- elected representatives drawn from county councils and
  borough councils; these account for more than half the
  membership

Table 5.1: Counties comprising and population of health board areas in 1991

Health board	Counties	Total population
Eastern	Dublin Kildare Wicklow	1,244,000
North Eastern	Cavan Louth Meath Monaghan	300,000
South Eastern	Waterford Carlow Kilkenny Tipperary (SR) Wexford	383,000
Midland	Laois Longford Offaly Westmeath	203,000
Southern	Cork Kerry	532,000
Mid-Western	Limerick Clare Tipperary (NR)	311,000
Western	Galway Mayo Roscommon	343,000
North Western	Donegal Leitrim Sligo	208,000

• professional representatives of the medical, nursing, dental and pharmaceutical interests who are mostly officers of the board
• nominees of the Minister for Health of which there are three on each board.

Each health board has a chief executive officer who is

responsible for day-to-day administration. The chief executive officer has, by statute, personal responsibility for the appointment, control and remuneration for staff and for deciding on the entitlement of individuals to health services. In addition, he may be delegated authority from the board to perform other functions. Policy decisions on services and expenditure, however, are the responsibility of the board.

Management
The blueprint for the development of the management of the health services after 1970 is contained in the report prepared by McKinsey and Co., management consultants, entitled *Towards Better Health Care – Management in the Health Board*. It proposed a management team headed by a chief executive officer with a team of six or four, depending on the size of the health board area, and including programme managers and functional officers. The management team concept replaced the hierarchical system which was a feature of the county management system of administration and is based on patient care needs rather than geographical areas.

Other bodies
As part of the administrative organisation of the health services under the Health Act, 1970, the following bodies were established in addition to the health boards – Comhairle na nOspidéal, three regional hospital boards (based in Dublin, Cork and Galway) and local advisory committees.

The functions of Comhairle na nOspidéal include the regulation of the number and type of consultant medical and certain other staff in the hospitals, and advising the Minister for Health on matters relating to the organisation and operation of hospital services.

The regional hospital boards, whose establishment had been recommended in the *Report of the Consultative Council on the General Hospital Services* (1968), were charged with the general organisation and development of hospital services in an efficient manner by the health boards and voluntary organisations. They were not to be concerned with the day-to-day running of the hospitals. The areas covered by these boards were intended to be three regions, each comprised of a number of health board regions; for example, the Galway-based regional hospital board was to encompass the Western and North-Western Health Board areas. These boards were never fully activated, however, and in 1977 the National Health Council[5] called for their abolition.

The 1970 Health Act also made provision for another body, the local advisory committee, which would function on a county basis and would have an advisory role together with any function delegated by the health board. Membership of this committee was made up of local councillors, the county manager, members of the medical profession and representatives of voluntary social service organisations. These committees were abolished in 1988.

In relation to the health board structure, the Department of Health in its document *Health: The Wider Dimensions*, stated:

> Given the size of the country and the population, the need for eight separate administrations, each with statutory responsibility for providing the whole range of health and personal social services, has also been questioned.[6]

The Department did not, however, indicate how many health boards there should be nor did it suggest an alternative structure.

Finance

The major source of income for expenditure on health services at present is the exchequer; up to 1977, however, local taxation was an important and significant source of income.

During the nineteenth century local rates constituted the primary source of income for health services and only towards the end of the century was state aid provided. By 1947, state grants accounted for 16 per cent of the total cost of the services. Post-war developments in the health services necessitated increased state expenditure. Under the Health Services (Financial Provisions) Act, 1947, the state undertook to meet for each health authority the increase in the cost of its services over what that authority had spent in the base year (the financial year ended 31

March 1948), until the cost of the services provided by the authority was being shared equally with the exchequer. The White Paper of 1966 indicated that local rates were not a form of taxation suitable for collecting revenue on the scale required for proposed developments in the health services and recommended instead that the cost of further extensions of the services should not be met by the local rates. By 1970, the exchequer's contribution amounted to 56 per cent of total costs. In 1973 the government decided to remove health charges from local rates over a four-year period and by 1977 the transfer had been completed.

Another source of revenue for health services was introduced under the Health Contributions Act, 1971. This was introduced at the request of the Department of Finance which was concerned at the falling contribution from local rates. Up to 1991 the contribution made by individuals was based on a percentage of earnings subject to an income limit which was usually adjusted upwards on an annual basis. In 1991, however, the income limit was abolished and the contribution (1.25 per cent) is now levied on total income.

Another source of income since 1973 is derived under EC regulations. These receipts are mainly in respect of health services provided for people for whom Britain is liable under EC regulations. They include recipients of British pensions, dependants of people employed in Britain and British holiday-makers.

The Hospitals Trust Fund was an important source of revenue for hospitals for several decades. A number of voluntary hospitals joined forces to run a sweepstake from horse racing in 1930. The venture proved successful and under the Public Hospitals Act, 1933, available surpluses of ensuing sweepstakes were to be payable to the Hospitals Trust Fund, appointed by the Minister for Local Government and Public Health to administer the funds. The income from the Fund was used mainly for capital expenditure on all hospitals. Up to 1974, voluntary hospitals were financed by capitation grants from the Department of Health and grants from the Hospitals Trust Fund towards revenue deficits. The role of the Hospitals Trust Fund in financing hospital development and services had declined considerably in importance when the sweepstake was abolished in the early 1980s. It had, however, made a substantial contribution to the development of hospitals. Barrington has noted that:

> The availability of sweepstake money enabled a level of investment in hospitals which, arguably, could not or would not have been provided otherwise.[7]

Almost 90 per cent of funds for health services are now derived from the exchequer (Table 5.2).

Table 5.2: Sources of finance for statutory non-capital health services, 1991

	£m	%
Exchequer	1,441,726	88.4
Health contributions and miscellaneous	147,384	9.0
Receipts under EC regulations	41,890	2.6
Total	1,631,000	100.0

Source: Department of Health, *Health Statistics*

Services
The work of health boards is divided into three broad programmes, each with a programme manager. The programmes are: Community Care, General Hospital, Special Hospital. These provide a useful framework for an examination of health services.

Community Care Programme
The traditional pattern of health services in Ireland placed great emphasis on institutional care. The policy in recent decades, however, has been to emphasise community rather than institutional services. The Community Care Programme aims to provide and develop services in the community as opposed to within an institutional setting. The basic reasoning behind this is that it is justified on social as well as economic grounds and than an efficient community care health service will reduce the demand for hospital beds. There is now a widespread acceptance of the

concept of delivering services, outside the hospital programmes, through community care teams which include
representatives of the different disciplines involved in
community care. While the term 'community care' has now
gained general acceptance and usually refers to non-
institutionalised care, it is open to different definitions and
interpretations. The NESC pointed out that community
care:

... entails an active role for the state in providing a framework of services to families, communities and voluntary
organisations to allow them to provide various forms of
care.[8]

The McKinsey Report recommended that teams be drawn
from all those engaged in field services including doctors,
nurses, dentists, social workers, health inspectors and
assistance officers. They would bring to bear on the
problems of the family or the individual the concerted
efforts of a team rather than the fragmented work of
individuals from different services. This system would lead
to the devolution of services, the discontinuance of centralised specialist groupings and the formation of new multi-
disciplinary teams, each to be headed by a director of
community care. In 1977, health board regions were divided
into a number of community care areas, each with a
population of 100,000 to 120,000 with a community care
team and a director of community care. In many instances,
these community care areas conformed to county boun-
daries. On the basis of population in the Eastern Health
Board area, the region was divided into ten community care
areas – Kildare and Wicklow remaining as entities themselves, with Dublin being divided into eight areas.

The Community Care Programme covers a wide range of
services and has three sub-programmes: community protection, community health and community welfare services.

Community protection includes prevention of infectious
diseases, child health examinations, health immunisation,
health education and other preventive services.

Community health services include general practitioner
services, refund of drugs scheme, home nursing services,
dental, ophthalmic and aural services.

Community welfare includes a range of cash payments (e.g. disabled person's maintenance allowance, domiciliary care allowance for handicapped children), home help service, grants to voluntary welfare organisations, child care services.

The general practitioner service under the Community Care Programme is part of the General Medical Services (GMS), which accounts for 40 per cent of expenditure on the total Community Care Programme. It is, therefore, appropriate to briefly examine the nature of this particular service.

General Medical Services

As already noted, a free general practitioner service for poor persons was provided from 1851 in local dispensary districts. This system continued until the 1970 Health Act provided for its abolition. The White Paper of 1966 had referred to the advantages of the dispensary system but indicated that the segregation of the population into fee-paying patients (who attended the doctor's surgery) and public patients (who attended the dispensary) outweighed any of its merits.[9] Consequently, the 1970 Health Act provided for the introduction of a choice-of-doctor scheme under which eligible persons would not be discriminated against in regard to place of treatment. The choice-of-doctor scheme comes under the General Medical Services, which also subsumes the service provided by pharmacists to those eligible.

Following negotiations between the Minister for Health and the medical profession, the choice-of-doctor scheme was introduced in 1972. The scheme gave eligible patients, i.e. medical card holders and their dependants, the choice-of-doctor to the greatest extent practicable and ended the discrimination and stigma attached to the dispensary system. The introduction of the choice-of-doctor scheme has been described, with considerable justification, as 'a major landmark in the history of social development in Ireland'.[10] In 1990 there were almost 1,600 doctors and over 1,000 pharmacists participating in the scheme. Most of the doctors care for both private and eligible patients, although the ratio between both categories of patients may vary considerably between parts of the country since there is a wide divergence in the distribution of medical card holders. Up to 1989 participating doctors were paid a fee per consultation in accordance with a scale, which varied depending on the time at which the service was given and, in the case of domiciliary consultation, on the distance travelled.

Under the dispensary system, most of the doctors supplied drugs, medicines and appliances to eligible patients. Under the GMS, retail pharmaceutical chemists, who have entered into agreement with health boards, are the primary channel of supply of drugs prescribed for eligible persons. Prescriptions are dispensed without charge to the patient and the pharmacist recoups the cost of the drugs and in addition is paid a dispensing fee by the health board. In some rural areas where the doctor's practice is located at a considerable distance from the nearest retail pharmacist participating in the scheme, the doctor may dispense the medicines and is paid a dispensing fee for each patient.

Since its inception in 1972, expenditure on the GMS has been a matter of some concern, especially the cost of providing drugs and medicines which have accounted for about two-thirds of the total expenditure on the GMS annually. In 1975 the Minister for Health established a working party to examine prescribing patterns. Its report noted that a number of doctors overprescribed to a significant extent. This consisted in prescribing too many items, prescribing excessive quantities, and constantly prescribing the more expensive drugs without regard to their cost.[11]

A further working party, established by the Minister for Health in 1982, examined methods by which the GMS might be made more cost-effective, with a special emphasis on the way in which doctors were paid.[12] Under a new system of payment introduced in 1989 participating doctors receive a capitation payment in respect of each panel patient, weighted by reference to demographic characteristics (age and sex), and geographic factors (distance of the doctor's principal place of practice from the patient's home). Furthermore, fees are paid for a number of specified procedures. The Irish College of General Practitioners had criticised the fee-per-item system prior to its replacement on the grounds that:

... the GP's income depends solely on the number of face-to-face consultations which can be fitted into each day. It medicalises minor illness and induces unhealthy doctor dependence in the patient.[13]

Under the fee-per-item method of payment, there was also an observed relationship between the incidence of consultation and the level of prescribing, i.e. the greater the number of visits to doctors the greater the number of prescriptions. Under the new capitation-based system of payment, the incentive to overvisiting should be removed and it should also reduce prescribing rates by discouraging unnecessary consultation. However, the Commission on Health Funding has noted that a capitation system carries the potential disadvantage of undervisiting, since the doctor's payment in respect of each patient is fixed irrespective of the number of consultations. The Commission, therefore, emphasised the importance of monitoring the operation of the scheme to ensure that the change to a largely capitation-based system does not lead to inadequate or poorly targeted services.[14]

As a further means of making the GMS more cost-effective a National Drugs Formulary was introduced in 1991, having been drawn up by the Department of Health and the Irish Medical Organisation. The Formulary consists of a list of drugs and medicines selected for their cost-effectiveness, and while it is not mandatory on general practitioners, those participating in the GMS undertake, through their contract, to cooperate in its operation.

In summary, it is envisaged that the recent changes introduced in the GMS (methods of payments for doctors and National Drugs Formulary) will bring about a more cost-effective service.

Other community care services

The NESC examined a number of community care services and concluded that wide variations in the level of services for children, the elderly, and the handicapped could be attributed to the lack of national guidelines on the appropriate level of service, the lack of national uniform criteria of eligibility for certain services, and the discretionary nature of some services.[15]

The NESC also noted the remarkable level of agreement that community care is a desirable objective as affirmed in various official policy documents over the past few decades. However, the implications of this objective have not been specified in terms of services required, nor has there been a commitment to make the necessary resources available. The development of community care, according to the NESC, has been hindered by organisational problems. Thus, for example, the teams envisaged by McKinsey have not functioned satisfactorily in all areas.

General Hospital Programme
This programme covers the treatment of patients in medical, surgical and maternity hospitals, including treatment and outpatient consulting clinics associated with these hospitals. These services are provided either directly by health boards in hospitals under their control or by contract with voluntary and private hospitals. There are three categories of hospitals: public, voluntary public and private.

Public hospitals evolved from the workhouses of the nineteenth-century Poor Law. Following the abolition of the workhouses in the 1920s, a county system of hospitals was established.

Voluntary public hospitals, some of which date from the early eighteenth-century, are run largely by religious orders. They are confined mainly to the larger urban areas, especially Dublin where the greatest demand for services existed and where financial support for their upkeep was also likely to be more readily available. These hospitals are now funded directly by the Department of Health. A number of them were closed in the late 1980s.

Private hospitals are mostly run by religious orders and some share the same complex with voluntary public hospitals (e.g. the Mater Private Hospital and the Mater Hospital). These private hospitals do not receive direct state subsidies.

Given the manner in which the hospital system evolved over a period of time it is not surprising that rationalisation would have become an issue, especially when the health services in general were being subjected to scrutiny in the 1960s.

In 1967, the Minister for Health, Seán Flanagan, appointed a consultative council with the following terms of reference:

> To examine the position in regard to general hospital inpatient and outpatient services in the state and to report in outline on the future organisation, extent and location of these services ... so as to secure ... that the public is provided in the most effective way with the best possible services.

The chairman of the council was Professor Patrick Fitzgerald and the report is usually referred to as the Fitzgerald Report.[16] In general, the report indicated that the existing hospital system was defective in staffing, equipment, quality of service and teaching standards. It suggested that the system could only be improved by a radical reorganisation involving, among other things, a considerable reduction in the number of centres providing acute treatment and a planned and coordinated hospital organisation embracing both the public and voluntary hospitals. It recommended that the hospital system be reorganised into three regions based on the medical teaching centres in Dublin, Cork and Galway. Each region would have a regional hospital of 600-1,000 beds offering a full range of services supported by a number of general hospitals of about 300 beds throughout the region. The existing district hospitals would be staffed by general practitioners catering for non-acute cases needing care. The existing county hospitals were to be community health centres providing inpatient services as suggested for district hospitals but backed by increased diagnostic facilities and a more comprehensive consultant outpatient organisation.

There was no official commitment to implement the recommendations of the Fitzgerald Report, and in 1973 the Minister for Health initiated a process of widespread consultation, involving the medical profession, health boards, and Comhairle na nOspidéal. Guidelines drawn up by Comhairle modified the earlier recommendations of the Fitzgerald Report and proposed, among other things, that the general aim should be to organise acute hospital services with specified minimum staffing so that the population served would be within a radius of thirty miles of the hospital centre. The Minister accepted the Comhairle guidelines as a reasonable basis for improving the hospital service and for decisions on the future system.

Following a process of consultation with all of the interested parties, the General Hospital Development Plan (GHDP) was announced by the Minister for Health, Brendan Corish, in October 1975. It differed fundamentally from the Fitzgerald Report in the number of acute care hospitals to be established. The GHDP envisaged the development of general hospitals in twenty-three locations (about twice as many as envisaged in the Fitzgerald Report) and speculated on a further number of community hospitals in formats and locations to be decided upon. The plan contained no detail of the future development of hospital services in either Cork or Limerick cities beyond tentative mention of the possibility of a major hospital service in the north-east area of Cork city. In addition, decisions in some other cases were postponed pending further consultation. The major differences between the GHDP and the Fitzgerald Report were distance of population from a general hospital (thirty miles versus sixty miles) and, related to that, the number of centres in which general hospitals should be located (twenty-three versus twelve).

The GHDP could be viewed as a balance between professional medical opinion and broader political considerations. The editorial in *The Irish Times* commented at the time:

> Indeed, it is not so much a national plan of any substance as an interim political statement on the state of play at local level.[17]

In its pre-election manifesto of 1977, the Fianna Fáil party included an undertaking 'to preserve the role of the county hospital in providing the necessary level of services for the local community'.[18]

Since the GHDP was not comprehensive and in the absence of a detailed policy statement from the new government, Comhairle na nOspidéal concluded that the country would in the future be served by a limited number of large specialised hospitals in Dublin, Cork and Galway (at least seven and possibly nine), and by a large number of smaller general hospitals (about twenty-four or twenty-six). Comhairle indicated that:

Inherent in such a situation of many small hospitals is the danger that medical deficiencies, spelled out in the Fitzgerald Report and for which that body proposed medical solutions, will continue to exist.[19]

It was largely in the context of cutbacks in public expenditure on the health services that a rationalisation of hospitals occurred in the late 1980s (Table 5.3). During this period a number of the public voluntary hospitals and the smaller public district hospitals were closed, often amid considerable controversy. The most notable example was that of Barrington's Hospital in Limerick, a public voluntary hospital which had been established under charter in 1830. The proposal by the Department of Health to close this hospital gave rise to vehement public opposition with an estimated 20,000 persons attending a demonstration in Limerick city in January 1988 to protest against the closure. It also led to the government being defeated on a Private Member's motion in the Dáil in February 1988. The defeat briefly raised the prospect of a general election, but the motion was not binding on the government and the hospital closed in the following month.

The number of acute care hospitals and consequently the number of beds have been reduced, especially since the mid-1980s (Table 5.3). It is highly questionable, however, that this occurred as a result of any coherent national plan.

Table 5.3: Numbers, numbers of beds and average duration of stay in acute hospitals, 1980-1991

	No. of hospitals	No. of beds	Average duration of stay (days)
1980	157	19,183	9.7
1984	152	18,857	7.5
1987	121	15,225	7.3
1989	103	13,709	7.3
1991	104	13,806	6.8

Source: Department of Health, *Health Statistics*

In practice, the closures were brought about by a combination of the Department of Health reducing budgets to health boards, leaving them with no option but to close the smaller hospitals, and simply informing public voluntary hospitals, which it funded directly, that they would have to close. This absence of national planning led the chief executive of a health board to comment in 1987:

> The area of greatest cost in health is the acute hospital service, and it is the service where intelligent planning is most required. But we have no national plan for general hospitals and no national political willingness to provide one. It is very hard for members of health boards to face up to hard political choices when their seniors in government at national level have for so long successfully avoided making such decisions themselves.
>
> We have had our chances at this in the past but the truth is that at national level we chickened on it. In 1975, following long and widespread consultation the then Minister, Brendan Corish, published a national plan for acute hospitals, under which 22 centres would be developed and 10 or 11 acute hospitals would be used as community hospitals. Twelve years later the hospitals which were to go have all been upgraded at considerable expense and now we are being told nationally we have too many acute hospitals and must reduce them. The cuts this year were directed by the Minister specifically at acute hospitals. In the absence of an agreed national plan the effect will be to downgrade all our acute hospitals and instead of a limited number of good hospitals we will have a larger number of poor hospitals.[20]

Special Hospital Programme
The Special Hospital Programme covers services for the psychiatrically ill and the mentally handicapped.

Psychiatric services
For many decades the focus of care in relation to psychiatric illness was the psychiatric hospital. More recently, however, there has been a decline in the number of patients in such hospitals and there is now far greater emphasis on a range of community services. Inpatient treatment is provided in health board psychiatric hospitals, units

attached to general hospitals, and a small number of private psychiatric hospitals.

In 1961 a Commission of Inquiry on Mental Illness was appointed to examine and report on the health services available for the mentally ill and to make recommendations on the measures required to improve these services. The Commission's report, published in 1966, indicated that in 1961 there were 7.3 psychiatric beds per 1,000 of the population, which appeared to be the highest in the world.[21] No clear explanation emerged for the exceptional rates of residence in psychiatric hospitals here but the Commission suggested a possible combination of reasons: high rate of emigration, low marriage rates, unemployment, social and geographic isolation in rural areas, and unhelpful public attitude towards mental illness which hinders discharge.

In 1981 the Medico-Social Research Board took a census of patients in psychiatric hospitals. Among the important findings of that census were that approximately one-third were over sixty-five years of age, a very high proportion (79.5 per cent) were unmarried, and one-fifth were resident in hospitals for twenty-five years or more.[22]

Another major review of psychiatric services was carried out by a study group between 1981 and 1984. Its report, *The Psychiatric Services: Planning for the Future*, provided a new planning framework for the development of a community based psychiatric service.[23] The report was widely welcomed. In summary, the report set out guidelines for future development, as far as possible in a community setting, with the emphasis on resources being transferred from large psychiatric hospitals to a range of alternative community based services and to acute general hospitals. Among the key elements in the planning framework were:

- the location of services close to where people work and a strong emphasis on outpatient and day care
- the provision of inpatient treatment in psychiatric units in general hospitals, with the role of the traditional psychiatric hospitals diminishing as alternative community based services are developed
- the provision of high support hostels for a small number who will require long-term inpatient care and the provision of appropriate housing in the community

- services to be provided on a sectoral basis for a given population by a multi-disciplinary team to be based in each sector.

The report proposed the gradual dismantling of psychiatric institutions and their replacement, as far as possible, by community based services. This approach is in keeping with the general emphasis on community care and the move away from institutional care. The Commission on Health Funding stressed the importance of ensuring that community support services are in place for psychiatric patients discharged from institutions. It stated that:

> The discharge of patients to inadequate care, as has occurred in some countries, is an abdication of society's responsibility to the most vulnerable of its members, creates fear and distrust in the population generally and leads to additional costs for other public services.[24]

Though the report of the study group is being implemented some voluntary organisations have noted that while patients are being discharged from psychiatric hospitals, adequate community support services are not being provided and the voluntary sector is being left to bear the burden.

The *Green Paper on Mental Health* (1992) stated that:

> In most health boards there are some psychiatric services which are comprehensive and community-oriented as defined in *Planning for the Future*, but such services are still not the norm.[25]

The Green Paper also noted that the psychiatric hospital still plays a major role in the psychiatric service but that this role is diminishing and changing. An increasing number of day and community facilities are providing an alternative to long-term care in psychiatric hospitals. This trend is reflected in the continued fall in the number of patients in psychiatric hospitals and the increase in places in day hospitals, day centres and hostels during the 1980s (Table 5.4).

Mental handicap
In 1961, a Commission of Inquiry on Mental Handicap was appointed to examine and report on the arrangements for

Table 5.4: Trends in psychiatric provision, 1984-1990

	Public psychiatric hospitals		Day hospitals and centres		Hostels	
	Admissions	No. of patients	No.	Places	No.	Places
1984	28,330	11,613	32	800	121	900
1990	22,118	7,817	97	2,424	292	2,081

Source: Green Paper on Mental Health (1992), chapter 2

the care of the mentally handicapped. The Commission's report, published in 1965, stated that as in many other countries the development of most of the specialist services for the mentally handicapped in Ireland had been of comparatively recent origin.[26]

The current emphasis in relation to policy on mental handicap is the development of community based alternatives to institutional care. At present persons with mental handicap are catered for in different institutional settings, i.e. psychiatric hospitals, special residential centres, hostels and supervised lodgings, and there is an increasing emphasis on day care provision (see pp. 157-64).

Programme structure
Despite the increased emphasis on the importance of community care, expenditure patterns in the health services do not reflect any noticeable shift towards community care services as opposed to hospital services (Table 5.5). Part of the reason for this is that hospital based services have a high profile, both politically and among the public at large. There are considerable difficulties associated with the rationalisation of hospital services as has already been indicated. Furthermore, there appears to be a lack of clear-cut policy objectives in attaining levels of community based services.

The Department of Health in a document published in 1986, *Health: The Wider Dimensions,* indicated that due to the programme structure, little incentive existed within health board areas for integrated planning of services across care programmes, based on measured health needs. It therefore proposed a change to geographical area rather than care programmes as the unit of management. In other words, it proposed a structure somewhat similar to that which existed prior to the 1970 Health Act where all health services in a geographic area were managed in an integrated manner.

Expenditure by programme
Half of current expenditure goes on the general hospital programme while the combined community care sub-programmes account for one-quarter (Table 5.5). Despite increased emphasis on the value and importance of community care and some rationalisation of hospital services, this pattern of expenditure has not altered significantly over the past two decades.

Table 5.5: Gross* non-capital expenditure on health services, 1991

Programme	*£(000s)*	*%*
Community Protection Programme	26,210	1.5
Community Health Service Programme	260,780	14.8
Community Welfare Programme	140,500	8.2
Psychiatric Programme	183,390	10.4
Programme for the Handicapped	164,920	9.4
General Hospital Programme	897,060	51.2
General Support Programme	79,140	4.5
Total	1,752,000	100.0

* When income from charges and other sources is taken into account the net non-capital expenditure was £1,631 million.

Source: Department of Health, *Health Statistics*

Eligibility for health services
From June 1991, the population has been divided into two categories for eligibility for health services. In summary, the lowest income group, i.e. medical card holders and their dependants, accounting for 35 per cent of the population, are entitled to all health services free of charge; the remainder are entitled to a more limited range of services. The main difference between the two groups is that while the medical card population is entitled to a free general practitioner service and hospital service (in public wards of

public and voluntary public hospitals), the rest of the population is liable for general practitioner fees but is entitled to a free hospital service on the same basis as the medical card population. Prior to 1991 the system was highly complex with the population divided into three categories. This situation had evolved over a considerable period of time. Thus, since 1851 the low income group had eligibility for health services and in 1953 the middle income group obtained limited eligibility for services, leaving the higher group basically without any entitlement. In 1979 further reforms were introduced to simplify the system of eligibility but the three-tiered system remained until 1991.

Medical cards
Persons with full eligibility for health services are defined in the 1970 Health Act as 'adult persons unable without undue hardship to arrange general practitioner, medical and surgical services for themselves and their dependants and dependants of such persons'. Those with full eligibility receive a General Medical Services card (medical card) which entitles them to free health services. Each health board keeps a register of persons with full eligibility which is updated regularly. Prior to the establishment of health boards the criteria used in assessing means were not uniform in all administrative areas.

Since 1974, however, the chief executives of health boards have jointly agreed on general guidelines which have been used in determining those categories which have full eligibility. These guidelines have no statutory effect and are issued primarily to inform each health board and the public in general of the broad categories of persons who normally qualify for full eligibility. Entitlement to a medical card is based on assessment of means and the means test is carried out by community welfare officers of health boards. In practice, means tests are not carried out on recipients of certain social welfare payments who have already been means tested. Each year health boards issue annual income limits for eligibility for medical cards.

Since the improvements in the GMS with the introduction of the choice-of-doctor scheme in 1972, the number of persons with medical cards and the total number covered by medical cards, i.e. medical card holders and their dependants, increased up to the late 1980s (Table 5.6). There are now 1.2 million covered by medical cards, representing 35 per cent of the total population. A number of factors account for the increase throughout the 1970s and early 1980s. Firstly, the takeup of medical cards would have increased as a result of the abolition of the dispensary system to which a certain stigma was attached. Secondly, the introduction of uniform guidelines to determine eligibility for medical cards would also have led to an increase in takeup. Thirdly, during this period there was an increase in the social welfare population mainly due to the increase in unemployment and thus, by definition, there was an increase in the lower income group.

There is considerable variation between health boards in relation to the proportion of the population covered by medical cards. These differences broadly reflect income variation within the country. Thus, in 1991 the North-Western Health Board had the highest proportion of population covered by medical cards (48.4 per cent) while the Eastern Health Board had the lowest (28.7 per cent). It should be noted also that while there are uniform income guidelines for determining eligibility for medical cards, this does not necessarily mean that there is uniformity in the manner in which the means test is carried out between health boards. In this context the PESP promised a review of medical card eligibility to ensure uniformity and consistency between all health boards and that a medical card appeal system would be established.[27]

Table 5.6: Number of persons and percentage of population covered by medical cards, 1972-1991

	Number of persons	*% of total population*
1972	864,106	29.0
1976	1,193,909	37.0
1980	1,199,599	35.6
1986	1,326,048	37.4
1988	1,324,849	37.4
1991	1,237,772	35.1

Source: Reports of the General Medical Services (Payments) Board

Reference has already been made to the fact that the system of eligibility was highly complex up to June 1991. In fact, an attempt was made in 1974 to rationalise the system into two categories, as was done in 1991. The Minister for Health, Brendan Corish, announced in August 1973, that from April 1974 every member of the community would be entitled to free hospital inpatient and outpatient services. Because of the opposition of hospital consultants, however, regarding their conditions of employment, and remuneration in particular, the Minister was forced to defer the introduction of the scheme. The rationalisation in 1991 was announced in the PESP and on this occasion the opposition by hospital consultants was more muted.

Voluntary Health Insurance
The Voluntary Health Insurance Board (VHI) was established under the Voluntary Health Insurance Act of 1957 and is charged with providing a health insurance scheme. The VHI is a non-profit-making body and any surplus on its income is devoted to the reduction of insurance premiums or increases in benefits. The VHI was established essentially as a means by which those in the higher income group, who did not have eligibility to health services at the time would be able to insure themselves against the cost of medical care.

By 1958, one year after its establishment, 57,000 persons were covered by the VHI scheme. The numbers have increased steadily since then so that by 1991 there was a membership of 1,289,000 (36.6 per cent of the total population). For some time it was clear that the total membership of the VHI was in excess of the estimated number of people who, strictly speaking, should have taken out insurance to cover themselves against hospital charges, i.e. people in the former category 3 group or higher income group (see p. 136). In other words, persons with eligibility for free hospital services had also invested in supplementary cover to enable them to have private or semi-private accommodation and private treatment in hospitals. The rationalisation of the system of eligibility is unlikely to change this pattern.

Commission on Health Funding
The Commission on Health Funding was established by the

Minister for Health in June 1987 against a background of public expenditure cutbacks in the health services and growing disquiet among health service unions and the public at large with the consequences of these cutbacks. The establishment of the Commission must also be viewed against a background of reviews in other countries stemming from a concern with the performance of health services and in particular the efficient use of resources.

The Commission, under the chairmanship of Miriam Hederman-O'Brien, had as its term of reference:

> To examine the financing of the health services and to make recommendations on the extent and sources of the future funding required to provide an equitable and cost-effective public health service and on any changes in administration which seem desirable for that purpose.

The Commission's report was published in September 1989. The report examined not only the financing of the health services but also the administration and delivery of services, the quality of services, and the mix of public and private health care; it made appropriate recommendations. The Commission stated that:

> The kernel of the Commission's conclusions is that the solution to the problem facing the Irish health services does not lie primarily in the system of funding but rather in the way that services are planned, organised and delivered.[28]

The Commission's main recommendations and supporting arguments in relation to finance, eligibility, administration, and some other issues are summarised here.

Finance
The Commission concluded that the level of public health funding cannot be determined by reference to a fixed proportion of gross domestic product or by reference to international comparison. The level can only be decided in the context of the available resources and the priorities attached by Irish society to different social objectives.

The Commission referred to three main methods of funding health services, i.e. general taxation, social insurance, and private insurance. It pointed out that no country relies exclusively on any one of these approaches. The majority of the Commission favoured public funding as the main funding method. It opted for this in preference to private funding for the following reasons:

- It would achieve a greater degree of comprehensiveness since the state as central funder is favourably placed to plan and organise the delivery of a unified, integrated service for all categories of patient.
- The implementation of policy shifts, such as the transfer of resources from institutional to community care, can be more easily achieved when there is a single major health funder.
- Equity of contribution towards the cost of services can be achieved by way of progressive taxation or social insurance.
- Equity of access can be controlled administratively to ensure that necessary services are available to all on the basis of need.

The majority felt that a private funding model would not be *equitable* (there could be discrimination against high risk groups), *comprehensive* (arising from problems in enforcing mandatory health insurance) or *cost-effective* (the international evidence suggests that cost control is not more successful under a private funding model).

Having opted for a public funding model, the choice was then between general taxation and a compulsory health insurance/earmarked tax system (linking the services provided with their cost). A majority favoured general taxation on the grounds that compulsory health insurance was effectively another tax, offering no real advantages over general taxation. The Commission recommended that the existing health contribution (1.5 per cent of all income from 1991) should be abolished. It pointed out that while local taxation was a major source of funding for health services in the past it should not be reintroduced for this purpose since it could hinder national planning of facilities.

Eligibility
The Commission argued that the public at large should have available to it a certain level of necessary health services,

including primary care, hospital care, long-term care and personal social services. It pointed out, however, that this did not necessarily mean that they should all be publicly funded, delivered by public agencies or provided free of charge. The Commission recommended that the lowest income group (medical card holders and their dependants) should remain eligible for all necessary health services free of charge. The rest of the population should be eligible for 'core' services. These services would include acute hospital care, long-term care and personal social services; welfare and continuing care services such as those for mothers and children, the elderly, the disabled and the psychiatrically ill (possibly with some charges for these services). The services to which everyone is already entitled, such as a service for infectious diseases, should remain universally available.

The Commission's recommendations regarding eligibility basically envisaged a two-tier system, i.e. the abolition of category 3 as then existed. This is similar to what was proposed in the *Programme for Economic and Social Progress*, which came into effect in June 1991.

The Commission also recommended that patients would have to opt for either public or private care and should not be allowed to combine them. Those opting for private care should pay the full costs involved.

The Commission recommended that the criteria for eligibility for medical cards should be uniform throughout the country so that people in similar circumstances would not be treated differently. Eligibility for all services, including discretionary services, should also be the same throughout the country and where charges for such services obtain they should also be uniform.

Administration
Under the existing structure the eight health boards have statutory authority to administer health services in their areas and they report to the Department of Health which overviews general policy and funding. This is necessarily a simplified and ideal model. The Commission identified a number of weaknesses in the actual operation of this structure:

• a confusion of political and executive functions

- lack of balance between national and local decision making
- inadequate information and evaluation systems
- inadequate accountability
- insufficient integration of services
- inadequate representation of the consumer viewpoint.

One of the main problems cited by the Commission is that many voluntary agencies providing health services are not funded by health boards and therefore do not report to them: instead they are funded directly by the Department of Health. These include voluntary hospitals which account for over half of acute hospital services and some of the larger voluntary organisations providing services for the handicapped. The Department of Health and the Minister for Health are consequently involved in the management of these services rather than concentrating exclusively on developing and monitoring policy. This is but one instance which has contributed to a situation where communication lines between the Department of Health and health boards are inevitably blurred. The Commission makes the general point that accountability in the system as between health boards and the Department lacks clarity. Similarly, the Commission also refers to health boards which by nature of their membership become unnecessarily involved in the management of services.

In order to overcome these weaknesses, the Commission recommended that a new structure be introduced along the following lines:

- The Minister for Health and the Department of Health should formulate health policy and should not be involved in the management of individual services. The range and quality of services and the eligibility for access to them should, as far as possible, be laid down by legislation.
- The management of the health services should be transferred to a new agency, the Health Services Executive Authority, which would be appointed by the Minister. The Authority would be responsible for the management and delivery of health and personal social services in the context of health policies set by the Minister for Health.

- A structure of area general managers, responsible to the Authority, should be established covering defined geographical areas in which the manager would be responsible for the delivery of services.
- Existing health boards would be abolished and replaced by health councils composed of elected representatives nominated by local authorities, whose function would be to represent local interests by influencing policy and by monitoring the quality and adequacy of local services. These councils would have limited powers to delay decisions of the area general managers.

The administrative changes proposed by the Commission on Health Funding are set out in Figure 5.1.

It has been argued by Joyce and Ham that the weaknesses identified by the Commission could be solved without establishing a Health Services Executive Authority or transforming health boards into health councils. They argued that health management is far more complex than that of other public services, and does not lend itself to a clear split between policy and execution as recommended by the Commission. It requires a political and professional input as is provided by the health board structure. They recommended:

> ... a strengthening of the Department's policy-making role, a clearer and greater delegation of function from the Department to the health boards, and a change in the statutory responsibility of health boards and the CEOs ... The purpose and mission of the health services must be clearly stated. National policy objectives for health must be developed.[29]

While the NESC supported the general diagnosis of the difficulties within the existing structure it did not accept that the Commission's proposed structure was entirely consistent with the diagnosis. Thus, for example, it was not clear, according to the NESC, how in retaining a political/representation function through health councils, the danger of local resistance to central policy and competition between regions for resources could be avoided. The NESC did not offer a definite view on a particular alternative structure.[30]

Figure 5.1: Health services administrative structure proposed by Commission on Health Funding

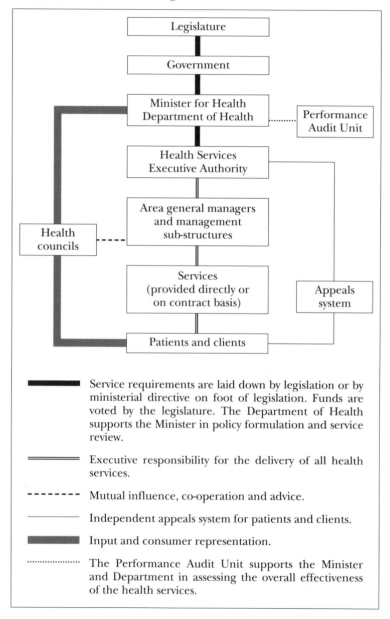

Source: Report of the Commission on Health Funding (1989), p. 162

Not surprisingly, members of health boards were united in their opposition to the administrative changes proposed by the Commission, arguing that the existing system had worked satisfactorily.[31]

In September 1991, the Minister for Health, Dr Rory O'Hanlon, referred to failings in the present health service structure as identified by the Commission on Health Funding and the Dublin Hospital Initiative Group, namely the lack of coordination between hospital and community based services, the resultant over-involvement of the Department of Health in day-to-day management issues, and the lost opportunities for achieving efficiencies through greater cooperation between agencies. The Minister indicated that the fragmentation of services and the lack of coordination was particularly acute in the Dublin area because of the multiplicity of autonomous agencies involved in the provision of health care. He therefore proposed to establish, through legislation, a single new authority which would be responsible for health and personal social services in the Eastern Health Board area; it would subsume the functions of the health board as well as some of the functions of the Department of Health. The Minister's proposals for the other seven health boards were less clear.[32]

The Minister may have accepted the diagnosis of the Commission on Health Funding but his remedy was different to the one prescribed.

Other issues
The Commission's proposals envisaged a continued mix of public and private care. The fundamental principle of the majority of the Commission was that it should not be necessary, nor should it be perceived as such, to take out private insurance in order to secure access to treatment. The role of private insurance therefore should be to provide cover for those wishing to avail themselves of private care and to provide cover for costs for which those without medical cards would be liable. The Commission was opposed to public subsidisation of private care when the state is already providing a core service to the entire population. It recommended that payments to the VHI should not qualify for tax relief (the cost of which in 1989

was £44 million), and that this relief, together with that of certain reimbursed medical expenses, should be phased out.

6

Welfare Services

Introduction

The basic social services, housing, education, health and income maintenance, cater for needs which are common to all members of society. However, certain groups have special needs, and services over and above the basic ones have evolved to cater for these needs. Such groups include the elderly, deprived children and the handicapped (both mentally and physically). While these groups are catered for to some extent by the basic services, special provision is also required. Hence services such as residential care for deprived children or sheltered employment for the handicapped have been developed.

It is in the field of welfare services that voluntary effort plays its greatest role. This is mainly because of the state's traditional preoccupation with providing satisfactory basic services for all members of society. In more recent years, however, state involvement in providing special provision for certain groups has improved and for this, voluntary organisations which frequently paved the way, must take some credit. Furthermore, voluntary organisations continue to play a leading role in the provision of social services.

This chapter examines the services for the elderly, the handicapped, and deprived children. It also examines the position of travellers in Irish society and, finally, the role of voluntary organisations in providing welfare services.

The elderly

The age at which a person may be said to be elderly or aged is an arbitrary one. However, it is usual to classify those aged 65 or over as elderly since this is the generally accepted age of retirement from employment.

147

A demographic feature common to most developed nations is the relatively high proportion of people aged 65 and over. This is mainly due to the reduction of mortality rates in infancy and childhood which has led to a considerable increase in life expectancy. The average life expectancy at birth in Ireland during the period 1925-27 was 57.4 for males and 57.9 for females. By 1989 these had increased to 71.0 and 77.0 respectively. In some European countries the proportionate increase in elderly persons is associated with a declining birth rate and a consequent proportionate decline in the younger age groups. In Ireland, similarly, the elderly had formed an increasing proportion of the total population up to the 1960s. In 1841, the proportion was approximately 3 per cent, and by 1961 this had increased to 11.2 per cent. While the absolute number of elderly persons has continued to increase, the percentage of such persons in the total population has remained relatively stable in the past few decades (see Table 6.1). This is largely explained by the general population increase in the same period.

The percentage of elderly persons varies considerably between urban (defined as towns containing populations of 1,500 or over) and rural areas of the state. In general, western counties have a relatively high proportion of elderly people compared with other counties. One of the principal reasons for the relatively high proportion of elderly persons in predominantly rural areas has been persistent migration. This migration has been selective in

Table 6.1: Number of persons aged 65 and over, 1926-1991

Year	Number	% of total population
1926	271,700	9.1
1936	286,684	9.6
1946	314,322	10.6
1961	315,063	11.2
1966	323,007	11.2
1971	329,819	11.1
1981	368,954	10.7
1991	394,830	11.2

Source: Census of Population

that members of the young adult age group have tended to migrate, leaving behind an imbalanced population structure with disproportionate numbers of elderly people.

A feature of the elderly population is the increasing proportion living alone. In 1966 there were 35,024 such persons, representing 10.8 per cent of all elderly persons. By 1981 these figures had increased to 68,034 and 18.4 per cent respectively. Those living alone are acknowledged to constitute a vulnerable group with potentially high demands on health and welfare services.

Growing concern over the increasing numbers of elderly persons and the inadequacy of existing services was recognised in 1965 when the Minister for Health, in consultation with the Ministers for Local Government and Social Welfare, appointed an inter-departmental committee whose function was 'to examine and to report on the general problem of the care of the aged and to make recommendations regarding the improvement and extension of services'. The report, entitled *The Care of the Aged*, was published in 1968. The recommendations of the report on improved services were, in the committee's view, 'based on the belief that it is better, and probably much cheaper, to help the aged to live in the community than to provide for them in hospitals or other institutions'.[1] The report reflected the then prevailing and increasing emphasis on community as opposed to institutional care.

In 1986 the Minister for Health, Barry Desmond, established a Working Party to review the existing health and welfare services for the aged. The Working Party's report, *The Years Ahead: A Policy for the Elderly*, was published in 1988.

Services for the elderly may be viewed under the two broad headings of community and institutional care.

Community care
The Care of the Aged report stressed the importance of providing adequate community support services. These would include income maintenance services, housing and general health and welfare services.

Income maintenance
There have been considerable improvements in the income

maintenance system for elderly persons over the last few decades. The main state income maintenance schemes are the contributory and non-contributory old age pensions. The former is paid to persons who have been in insurable employment and have made a sufficient number of contributions, while the latter is paid subject to a means test. The retirement pension, introduced in 1970, is also an insurance based scheme and applies to persons who retire from insurable employment at age 65; at age 66 they can revert to the contributory old age pension. There has been a substantial increase in the number of recipients of these pensions (Table 6.2). A notable feature of the pension population is the decline in the number of recipients of non-contributory pensions. This is due to the broadening of the social insurance base and the numbers should decline further as a result of the extension of social insurance to the self-employed in 1988. This group would have had to resort to the old age non-contributory pension in the past. In the 1970s the qualifying age for the old age pension was reduced from 70 to 66 years and the means test was eased. The effect of these measures was an increase in the number of recipients.

Table 6.2: Number of recipients of old age and retirement pensions, 1966-1991

Pension	1966	1978	1991
Old age contributory	40,556	61,838	72,764
Old age non-contributory	112,621	133,669	115,950
Retirement	–	29,585	52,236
Total	153,177	225,092	240,950

Several other improvements in the income maintenance system for elderly persons have been introduced, such as the living alone allowance (1977) and the age allowance. The report of the Commission on Social Welfare indicated that payments to the elderly were the highest of all social welfare groups and that they were closest to the minimally adequate income recommended by the Commission.[2] In a major survey, elderly persons expressed the highest level of satisfaction of any group with their income position.[3] However, *The Years Ahead* pointed out that: 'The general improvement in the income position of the elderly hides wide differences in income among the elderly themselves. The incomes of the elderly span a spectrum from the very wealthy to the very poor.'[4]

Housing
The elderly have benefited from a general improvement in housing over the past few decades. Since the early 1970s local authorities have allocated 10 per cent of new dwellings to the elderly and disabled. In some years this figure has been exceeded. In addition, local authorities, health boards and voluntary organisations have been involved in providing sheltered and special housing schemes for the elderly.

One of the features of the elderly population is that a very high percentage of them own their own dwellings. While there are few elderly in the private rented sector, most of those in the former rent-controlled dwellings were elderly persons.[5] Following the abolition of rent control in 1982, their interests, such as security of tenure, have been provided for in legislation. A special rent allowance scheme was introduced to ensure that they would not experience financial hardship because of the abolition of rent control and the subsequent increase in rents.

Despite these improvements it is still likely, however, that some of the worst living conditions and lack of household amenities exist in dwellings occupied by elderly persons.

Health and welfare services
A number of developments and improvements have occurred in the health and welfare services since the *Care of the Aged* report was published. These include the introduction of the choice-of-doctor scheme under the General Medical Services. A high proportion (over 80 per cent of elderly persons) are now in receipt of medical cards which entitle them to all basic health services free of charge. Domiciliary services for the elderly have also improved in recent decades. The public health nursing service, which involves domiciliary visiting, was extended in the 1970s and this has been accompanied by the

development of the home help service, meals on wheels and day care services for the elderly by health boards and voluntary organisations. The main beneficiaries of the home help service are elderly persons living alone. Despite improvements in the community health and welfare services, *The Years Ahead* indicated that less progress had been made in relation to the expansion of dental services, provision of physiotherapy and chiropody, the development of a social work service for the elderly, and the boarding out of elderly persons. In recommending that the home help service be improved, the report pointed out that just over 9,400 elderly persons were in receipt of this service and that despite its importance in maintaining the elderly at home in a cost-effective way, the evidence suggested that the service was in fact contracting.

The Years Ahead indicated that the developments which had occurred have resulted in substantial improvements in services for the elderly which have reinforced their independence and their ability to live at home. It also makes the point that the majority of elderly persons have an adequate income, own their homes, are active and independent and express considerable satisfaction with their lives. *The Years Ahead* classified the elderly population as follows:

- independent: 78 per cent
- dependent elderly at home: 17 per cent
- elderly in long-term care: 5 per cent

Institutional care
When the *Care of the Aged* report was published in 1968 a substantial number of elderly persons were in long-term care in county homes, some of which originated as Poor Law workhouses and catered for all categories of persons with very little assessment of their needs. In effect, they were catch-all institutions catering for a wide variety of elderly persons. The number of patients in these county homes, now referred to as geriatric hospitals, has declined and the accommodation and general standards have been improved. In line with the recommendation in the *Care of the Aged* report, a number of welfare homes were built for elderly persons who did not need full-time care in hospital but who could not live independently on their own at home. *The Years*

Ahead points out that, 'although the county homes have become geriatric hospitals, too much of the atmosphere of the older institution survives in some centres'.[6]

Extended care of the elderly is now provided in a variety of settings – health board geriatric hospitals and homes, district hospitals and welfare homes, voluntary hospitals, and voluntary and private nursing homes. During the early 1980s there was a decrease in the number of beds in health board hospitals and homes and a substantial increase in voluntary and private nursing home beds. The growth in nursing homes has been most apparent in the Eastern Health Board area where about half of all patients in private nursing homes are concentrated. The majority of the elderly in extended care are chronically ill but a significant proportion are in care for social reasons.

The Years Ahead recommended that existing geriatric hospitals/homes, long-stay district hospitals and welfare homes be developed, where appropriate, as community hospitals, i.e. hospitals which would provide a range of services including assessment, rehabilitation, convalescent care, day care, and respite care for relatives. In the larger urban areas, particularly Dublin, the report acknowledged that community hospitals would have to be purpose built.

The Years Ahead expressed concern about the general level of standards in private and voluntary nursing homes, the relationship between health boards and these homes, and the manner in which they were subvented. Notwithstanding existing legislative safeguards, it recommended that further measures should be adopted such as the introduction of a licensing system and the establishment of an independent inspectorate. The Health (Nursing Homes) Act of 1990 was introduced in response to the needs identified in *The Years Ahead*. The Act provides for the registration and inspection of homes, the introduction of regulations relating to the standards of care, and reform of the existing system of subvention to these homes.

Coordination
The key to the improved provision of services to the elderly is coordination. In this context *The Years Ahead* recommended the appointment of a district liaison nurse who would coordinate services in districts serving up to 30,000

people. It also envisaged the establishment of district teams made up of representatives of the different service providers (e.g. housing, health services). In each health board community care area (made up of several districts) there would be a full-time health official with a qualification as a community physician.

The recommendations of *The Years Ahead* imply the blurring of the traditional distinction between community and institutional services for the elderly; the model recommended is a continuum of care which is both flexible and responsible and in which residential care complements the supporting care in the community and in the family.

Child care services
This section is concerned with deprived children whose plight arises because they are orphaned, or more likely because the family has broken down, the parent or parents are unable to cope, or the children are involved in truancy or delinquency.

Up to the early 1970s the main statutory means of dealing with these children was to place them in residential care, i.e. in industrial schools or reformatories. Industrial schools dated from 1858 and were designed to cater for young children, while the reformatories, which originated in 1868, were for older delinquent children. These institutions were generally run by religious orders.

In 1970 a report on industrial and reformatory schools (usually referred to as the Kennedy Report after the chairman, District Justice Eileen Kennedy) was published. The key recommendation of this report was that:

> The whole aim of the child care system should be geared towards the prevention of family breakdown and the problems consequent on it. The committal or admission of children to residential care should be considered only when there is no satisfactory alternative.[7]

In 1980 the *Report of the Task Force on Child Care Services* was published. This report has its origins in 1974 following a government decision to allocate the main responsibility in relation to child care to the Minister for Health. The Minister established the Task Force to make recommendations on the extension and improvement of services for deprived children and to draw up a child care bill. The Task Force report also emphasised that as far as possible deprived children should be catered for in a family or community setting rather than in residential care.

Significant developments have occurred in relation to child care over the past few decades.[8] These are examined under the headings of services, administration and legislation.

Services
The philosophy underlining the Kennedy and Task Force Reports has, to some extent, been reflected in policy. The numbers in residential care have fallen and there has been an increased emphasis on the family support services. In 1968-69 there were 4,834 children in care (three-quarters in residential care and the remainder in foster care). By 1988 there were 2,614 children in care (just over one-quarter in residential care). With the establishment of health boards, social workers were employed under the Community Care Programme. Their primary focus is child care and child-centred family case work with an emphasis on keeping families together in their own homes as far as possible rather than resorting to alternative care. Where this is not possible, the preferred options are adoption or placement with foster parents, with residential care as a last resort.

Many of the industrial and reformatory schools have been closed since the early 1970s partly in response to the development of community services and in some instances because the religious orders involved decided, sometimes because of their own declining numbers, to opt out of this type of service. The residential centres now are based in many instances on group homes rather than the traditional large institutions. The terms 'residential home' and 'special school' have replaced those of industrial and reformatory schools respectively since the early 1970s. The funding of these homes is on a budget basis since 1984 as compared with the capitation system of the past. Furthermore, special courses have been provided for child care workers since the early 1970s.

The Kennedy Report had recommended that the Department of Health (rather than the Department of Education) should be responsible for all residential care facilities. This did not happen until 1982, but the Department of Education has retained responsibility for some special schools for severely deprived children.

Administration
The Kennedy Report and the Task Force Report refer to the fact that administrative responsibility for child care services was divided between three government departments – Health, Justice, and Education. Thus, for example, the Department of Health was responsible for personal and social services, while the Department of Justice administered the adoption service and juvenile justice system, and the Department of Education was responsible for the industrial and reformatory schools. Despite the fact that responsibility for developing child care services was assigned to the Department of Health in 1974, administrative responsibility still rests with three Departments, though their respective roles have changed somewhat. As already mentioned, for example, the Department of Education now has responsibility for a small number of special schools. The adoption service, formerly under the Department of Justice, was transferred to the Department of Health in 1983.

Both the Kennedy Report and the Task Force Report recommended that the Department of Health should have overall responsibility for all child services and the Task Force Report recommended that a child care authority be established at regional level. Both reports also recommended the establishment of an independent advisory body – the National Children's Council. Neither of these recommendations has been acted upon.

The division of administrative responsibility for child care services can lead to a situation where the type of care received depends on which of the statutory bodies first becomes aware of the plight of a particular child. Thus, for example, truancy (often symptomatic of more deep-seated problems in the family) is the responsibility of the school attendance service, which is part of the education system rather than the health service as the Task Force recommended.

Legislation
Until recently, the main legislation governing the child care

system was the Children's Act of 1908. The Kennedy Report recommended the introduction of a composite children's act and the terms of reference of the Task Force included the preparation of a new children's bill. This bill was not prepared by the Task Force.

In 1988 a Child Care Bill was introduced in the Dáil and was enacted in 1991. The main provisions of the Act include the following:

- Health boards are responsible for promoting the welfare of children (up to age 18) who are not receiving adequate care and protection.
- The power of health boards to provide child care and family support services is strengthened.
- Improved procedures for intervention where children are in serious danger.
- Revised provision for the inspection and approval of residential centres.

The *Programme for Economic and Social Progress* (1991) contains a commitment to implement the provisions of the Child Care Bill on a phased basis over seven years.

While the Adoption Act of 1988 introduced some limited reforms in that area and the Status of Children Act of 1987 abolished the legal concept of illegitimacy, there has not been any major legislative reform in the adoption and juvenile justice areas.

Despite the lack of progress in certain areas there has been considerable improvement in the quality and level of services provided for deprived children since the Kennedy Report.

The handicapped
Within the past few decades a number of reports concerned with the handicapped have been published. These include: *Report of Commission of Inquiry on Mental Handicap* (1965), *Report of the Working Party on Training and Employing the Handicapped* (1975), the NESC report, *Major Issues in Planning Services for Mentally and Physically Handicapped Persons* (1980), *Report of the Working Party on Services for the Mentally Handicapped* (1980), *Towards a Full Life: Green Paper on Services for Disabled People* (1984), *Report of the Review Group on Mental Handicap Services* (1991).

A handicap has been defined as:

A disadvantage for a given individual resulting from an impairment or a disability that limits or prevents fulfilment of a role that is normal (depending on age, sex and social and cultural factors) for that individual.[9]

This definition covers a wide range of disabilities and encompasses physical disabilities, mental handicap and long-term mental illness. A number of different disabilities come within the category of physically disabled, e.g. the deaf, the blind, those with speech difficulties and those with physical disabilities arising from congenital causes, accidents, or chronic or long-term illnesses. Similarly, the mental handicap category can also embrace a range related to the degree of handicap. It should be noted here that the Review Group on Mental Handicap Services (1991) indicated that the term 'mental handicap' should no longer be used and the Group adopted the designation 'moderate, severe or profound intellectual disability' while the term 'mild mental handicap' has been replaced with 'general learning difficulties'.

Numbers of handicapped
The Green Paper (1984) pointed out that there was no comprehensive source of information on the number of disabled persons. Information is available on the numbers of mentally handicapped and mentally ill but not on the physically disabled. The Green Paper estimated that the total number of disabled persons of all ages was 150,000.

The NESC report (1980) had stressed the need for a register of handicapped persons as a prerequisite to the planning of services. The Green Paper concurred with this and it proposed that the National Rehabilitation Board, in association with health boards, be responsible for the central administration, monitoring and future development of a records system for the physically handicapped. The Medico-Social Research Board (now the Health Research Board) had for some time been responsible for a mental handicap records system.

Services for the handicapped
Since issues related to psychiatric illness have already been

dealt with in Chapter 5 on the health services, the main focus here will be on services for persons with physical and intellectual disabilities.

A range of services exist for such persons. It is not possible to deal with all of these and only the more salient are examined together with trends in the provision of services.

The Green Paper states that:

There is no disagreement about the philosophy which should underpin the policies and progress for disabled people. The ultimate objective is to equip disabled people to realise their full potential and to participate to the greatest extent possible in the life of the community.[10]

Services for the physically handicapped
The health boards are responsible for a range of services for the physically handicapped, e.g. residential care and vocational training. The boards either provide these directly or, in practice, arrange for them to be provided by voluntary and private organisations.

One of the primary functions of the National Rehabilitation Board (established in 1967) is to advise the Minister for Health on all aspects of the rehabilitation of persons with disabilities. In addition, it is also involved with the provision of a range of specialised services for the assessment, counselling, vocational guidance, training and placement of people with disabilities.

While the state's involvement in the provision of services is considerable and has been growing in recent decades, voluntary organisations have made, and continue to make, substantial contributions in this area. There are several separate organisations specifically concerned with different types of disabilities, e.g. cerebral palsy, spina bifida, multiple sclerosis. Over forty of these organisations are affiliated to the Disability Federation of Ireland (formerly the Union of Voluntary Organisations for the Handicapped), an umbrella body which actively promotes the general welfare of people with disabling conditions.

Services for the mentally handicapped
The main initiative for the provision of services for the

mentally handicapped has come from voluntary organisations including religious orders, and parents' and friends'
associations. These organisations provide a range of services, e.g. residential care, training and day care centres,
and specialist services. Approximately 150 organisations are
affiliated to the National Association for the Mentally
Handicapped of Ireland, which promotes the general
welfare of mentally handicapped persons and disseminates
information on mental handicap.

The *Report of the Review Group on Mental Handicap Services*
estimated that the mental handicap population was approximately 25,000 and of these 13,000 have a moderate, severe
or profound degree of handicap. In 1988 over 11,000
persons were in residential, day care and training centres
(Table 6.3). The Review Group estimated that, at the minimum, a further 600 residential and 1,000 day places were
required to cater for accumulated and emerging needs,
transfer from inappropriate settings (such as psychiatric
hospitals) and further support services. It recommended
that these additional places be provided over four years
commencing in 1990.

Table 6.3: Type of provision for persons with intellectual disability, 1988

	Units	*Persons*
Residential centres	53	4,633
Hostels	212	1,184
Day care centres	87	1,913
Workshops/training centres	90	3,306
Total	442	11,036

Source: Report of the Review Group on Mental Handicap Services (1991), p. 65

Trends in service provision
In this section a number of trends related to the provision
of services in certain selected areas are outlined.

Education
In relation to education, the NESC report (1980) recommended that as far as possible handicapped children should
be educated with other children.[11] There are special classes

attached to ordinary schools and a number of special schools especially for mentally handicapped children. The official policy of the Department of Education is now one of integration of children with handicaps, where this is possible, while retaining the option of segregation where necessary. The *Report of the Primary Education Review Body* commented that there are limits to the degree of integration which is possible and that, in many instances, partial integration may be the only feasible option.[12]

Training and employment
Since the mid-1970s there has been increased emphasis on the training and employment of disabled persons. The *Report on Training and Employing the Handicapped* (1975) stated:

A great many handicapped persons are willing and able to work. Some require special training, others need special conditions of employment. The important thing is that no one should be denied the opportunity to work even if it requires a special effort by society to enable them to do so.[13]

The report recommended the establishment of community workshops with the dual function of training and sheltered employment. These workshops have been developed by the Rehabilitation Institute (established in 1949 as an independent voluntary body with its main focus on the provision of training facilities in over forty centres throughout the country), health boards and other voluntary organisations. They are intended to prepare persons with various disabilities for open employment while at the same time providing long-term sheltered employment for those who can achieve a reasonable level of production. The availability of finance from the European Social Fund has been an added stimulus to the provision of training for handicapped persons.

In 1977 the government introduced a quota scheme for the public service with a target of 3 per cent of jobs for disabled persons by the end of 1982. Over a decade later this target had not been reached and the extent to which progress had been made varied, with the record in the civil service exceeding that of local authorities, health boards and semi-state agencies.[14]

Institutional community services

Despite advances in medical care and community support services, it is recognised that a significant number of handicapped persons, especially mentally handicapped, will require long-term care. During the 1970s the main emphasis in the mental handicap services was on the development of residential facilities. These have been provided largely by voluntary organisations including religious orders and much of the capital for this development came from the Department of Health and health boards. During the 1980s, however, the emphasis was on providing a comprehensive network of services with a continuum of care. This would include sheltered housing, hostel accommodation, short-term residential care and a range of community support services.

A NESC report, *Community Care Services,* pointed out that four service areas relating to an enabling structure for community living for handicapped persons were identified in 1980 as in need of particular attention – domiciliary care, day care, support services including social work services, and rehabilitation services. The report pointed out that in terms of health board activity there had been very little change in any of these areas but that some domiciliary care initiatives had been undertaken by voluntary organisations. An example of the latter was a pilot day care attendance scheme, initiated by the Irish Wheelchair Association to give caring relatives some relief.[15]

Income maintenance

At present the Department of Social Welfare and the Department of Health administer income maintenance payments for handicapped persons. Thus, the Department of Social Welfare administers the blind pension, and health boards a blind welfare allowance. Health boards also administer the disabled person's maintenance allowance (in effect a long-term sickness assistance scheme), while the Department of Social Welfare administers the insurance-based disability benefit and invalidity pension.

The NESC report (1980) argued that only one agency should administer income maintenance payments.[16] The Green Paper was also critical of the lack of uniformity in the present payments system and, in recommending that the disabled person's maintenance allowance be transferred to the Department of Social Welfare, argued that the centralisation of administration would lead to a more consistent approach.[17] The Commission on Social Welfare also commented on the duplication of functions between the two government Departments and recommended that, in general, income maintenance payments should be the responsibility of the Department of Social Welfare.[18]

Access and mobility
The Green Paper pointed out that with few exceptions the physical surroundings have been designed for the active and healthy with little regard for the special needs of the disabled, the elderly, expectant mothers and others whose mobility is impaired or underdeveloped. It suggested that these problems arose more from insufficient understanding and awareness than from deliberate policy. There is now a greater awareness of the need to provide a barrier-free environment. From the early 1980s the Office of Public Works has been directed to ensure that all new buildings are fully accessible to the handicapped and to arrange modification and adaptation of existing buildings where possible. The Green Paper acknowledged that making the public transport system accessible was beset with difficulties both practical and financial.

Legislative safeguards
The Green Paper noted that while other countries have legislation to safeguard the rights of disabled persons it would need to be demonstrated clearly here that such measures would contribute in a practical way to an improvement in their conditions. It further stated:

> The most important thing which any disadvantaged minority needs is goodwill and understanding. The government are convinced that the promotion of the rights of disabled people can be best achieved by general agreement rather than by measures of compulsion.[19]

This conclusion was rejected by some organisations. For example, the Union of Voluntary Organisations for the Handicapped, in its response to the Green Paper, argued that a basic framework of rights should be set out in a Rights of Persons with Disabilities Act.[20]

The travelling people

A report on travelling people by the Economic and Social Research Institute in 1986 commented:

> The central conclusion of this study is an inescapable one: the circumstances of the Irish travelling people are intolerable. No humane and decent society, once made aware of such circumstances, could permit them to persist.[21]

This minority group is frequently the subject of popular criticism, prejudice and discrimination. Over the past few decades the number of travelling families has increased significantly and their general lifestyle has undergone considerable change. Up to the 1950s travellers were essentially rural based but since then there has been a gradual shift to urban areas as the basis of their activities in rural areas was undermined.

There have been two major official reports on travellers – *Report of the Commission on Itinerancy* (1963) and *Report of the Travelling People Review Body* (1983). In 1984 a Monitoring Committee was established by government and charged with monitoring the implementation of government policy and the provision of state services to travelling people. It has published an annual report since 1985. In addition, the Council for Social Welfare (a sub-committee of the Catholic hierarchy) has also published a report, *The Travelling People* (1985).

Some of the issues highlighted in these reports are examined here.

Definition

The Commission on Itinerancy defined an itinerant as:

> A person who had no fixed place of abode and habitually wandered from place to place, but excluding travelling show people and travelling entertainers.[22]

The Review Body pointed out that such a definition was inadequate because so many travellers had a permanent place to live. It used the term 'traveller' to designate membership of an identifiable group, pointing out that abandonment of the nomadic way of life does not automatically entail the renunciation of the traveller ethic nor integration with the settled community.[23] The term 'traveller' is the accepted one among travellers themselves.

Origins
The Commission stated that the existence of travellers in Ireland is ascribed to many causes, e.g. dispossession in various plantations, descendants of journeying craftsmen, eviction, famine. Some may be descendants of early poets and bards and craftsmen such as smiths and tanners. Others are likely to have originated in the period from the sixteenth to the nineteenth century when large numbers of peasants were either unable to meet their own subsistence needs or to pay the large rents demanded by landlords and were forced from the land. In addition, there may be other reasons why people adopted a nomadic lifestyle, e.g. as a result of personal social deviancy, such as alcoholism.[24]

Numbers
Censuses of travellers have been undertaken in various years. These years do not coincide with the normal census. Between 1960 and 1990 the number of traveller families more than trebled, from 1,198 to 3,542. Approximately one-quarter of families now live in the Dublin area.

Health status
Both the Commission and the Review Body indicated that travellers have a much lower life expectancy than the population in general and that the proportion of infant and child deaths to all traveller deaths is very high. Some of this is accounted for by the type of accommodation used by travellers and the health hazards associated with living on the roadside.

In 1987 the Health Research Board carried out a study of the health status of travellers. Among the findings were the following:

- Only 2 per cent of travellers were aged 65 or over as compared with 10.7 per cent of the total population.

- Life expectancy for male and female travellers is 62 years and 65 years, compared with 72 and 77 years for males and females generally.
- Travellers have a two and a half times greater chance of dying in a given year than settled people.
- The birth rate among travellers is over double the national rate, i.e. 34.9 per thousand as compared with 16.6.

The study concluded that:

The picture which emerges of the travelling people in 1987 from this report is of a group who marry at a very young age and have many children. From before birth to old age they have high mortality rates, particularly from accidents, metabolic and congenital problems, but also from the other major causes of death. Female travellers have especially high mortality compared to settled women. Those members of the travelling community who do not live in houses, approximately 50 per cent, have even higher mortality ratios than housed travellers, especially females and particularly from accidents.[25]

The Review Body recommended that health boards should provide special care and advice for travellers in relation to the care of mothers and children, availability of immunisation services, the treatment of handicapping conditions in children, and family planning, and should educate them as to the health hazards of caravans as permanent accommodation for a large family.

Education
The Commission on Itinerancy stated simply that almost all travellers were completely illiterate.[26] In 1960 only 160 children out of a total of 1,640 between the ages of 6 and 14 years were attending school. The Commission indicated that illiteracy accentuated the travellers' isolation from the settled population and in itself made all the more difficult any attempt to change over to the settled way of life. By 1980 much progress had been made, with about 3,500 children attending school (about half the total) in special classes or special schools which had been established. The Review Body noted, however, that progress to second level education was very rare and that there was little improve-

ment in the educational standards of adults, of whom about 90 per cent were illiterate.[27]

The *Fifth Report* of the Committee to Monitor the Implementation of Government Policy on Travelling People (1990) noted that there were four special primary schools and 143 special classes for travellers operating in primary schools throughout the country. The Committee commented that new measures were required to improve the participation levels of travellers' children at post-primary level. By 1989 there were twenty-seven special training centres throughout the country for young travellers. These centres are funded by FÁS and the Department of Education (through vocational education committees) and are established and operated with the involvement of the National Association of Training Centres for Travelling People. Out of a total of almost 500 travellers who completed the training programme in 1989, 298 went on to employment or further training.[28]

Employment
While there are some self-employed travellers, the majority are in receipt of unemployment assistance payments and there are relatively few in formal employment. This is due to a number of factors, e.g. illiteracy, lack of skills, and prejudice among employers. Many travellers are involved in scrap collection, which the Review Body considered a valuable service to the community. It recommended that facilities be provided for this purpose near their housing, or in special centres for heavy scrap.[29]

Settlement and accommodation
The Commission on Itinerancy recommended that:

> The immediate objective should be to provide dwellings as soon as possible for all families who desire to settle. Eventually the example given by those who successfully settle should encourage the remainder to leave the road.[30]

The Commission also noted that an overwhelming majority were in favour of settling. The Review Body noted that nothing that had happened since 1963 had lessened the correctness of the Commission's assessment. While much progress was made in providing housing for travellers (by 1990 approximately 1,700 families were in standard housing), the fact remains that in 1990 there were as many families on the roadside as thirty years previously (Table 6.4). The Review Body stated that while progress had been made there also had been failures and 'the greatest failure has resulted from the relative inaction of some local authorities who are slow in implementing government policy'.[31]

Table 6.4: Number of travelling families by type of accommodation 1960-1990

Type of accommodation	1960	1980	1990
Standard housing	56	957	1,471
Roadside	1,142*	1,149	1,146
Group/special housing	–	–	223
Chalets	–	253	71
Caravans on authorised sites	–	131	631
Total	1,198	2,490	3,542

*Includes 60 in motor trailers, 738 in horsedrawn caravans and 335 in tents.

The Review Body recommended that every local authority should provide a house for all traveller families in its area who want a house. Houses allocated should be individual houses or occasionally groups of houses for related families. In all cases they should be indistinguishable from houses for other tenants.

The Review Body also noted that the majority wished to live in houses (either alongside the settled community or in group housing), a minority in caravans on authorised sites with sanitary and other facilities, and a small number wanted to continue travelling but to have available authorised sites on which they could remain for as long as they wished. The settlement of travellers requires the commitment of local authority members and officials. Where they are favourable to the provision of housing or authorised sites they may come under intense pressure not only from the public (mostly residents' associations) but also from industrial and commercial interests. This has frequently resulted in plans being modified or abandoned.

The Committee to Monitor the Implementation of Government Policy on Travelling People in its annual report for 1989 was critical of the fact that some local authorities with significant numbers of traveller residents within their functional areas had for some time promised action to accommodate these families but had failed to do so.[32]

Relationships with settled community
Relationships between travellers and the settled population have been characterised by prejudice and discrimination on the one hand, and isolation on the other. The Review Body noted that: 'The general population of the country has very little detailed knowledge of travellers and the problems they face ... fear of travellers is in large measure groundless, where there is irrefutable evidence that those who settle in houses usually create no special problems.'[33]

The Review Body even considered the possibility of having special legislation enacted to outlaw discrimination against travellers but concluded, for various reasons, that this was not feasible.[34]

Role of voluntary organisations
In the 1960s a number of voluntary organisations, usually settlement committees, were established. In 1969 the first Council of Itinerant Settlement was set up and in 1973 this became the National Council for Travelling People. Some of the organisations also began to focus on educational projects. There has been a significant change in recent years in that travellers have begun to organise themselves, become politically active and lobby for their rights.[35] They have also been represented on various groups, such as the National Council for Travelling People, the Review Body, and the Monitoring Committee. In 1990 the National Council for Travelling People voted to disband itself. Arising from this, two organisations were set up – the National Federation of Irish Travelling People which aims to promote the general welfare of travellers, and the Irish Travellers' Movement which seeks to emphasise that travellers are a separate ethnic and cultural group.

Voluntary social service organisations
There is a strong tradition of voluntary activity in Ireland.

While this activity is widespread, its precise extent is not known. For example, there is no formal system of registration for charitable organisations although charitable status is granted to organisations by the Revenue Commissioners for tax purposes solely. The role of voluntary social service organisations is considerable in Ireland especially if it includes the role of religious orders whose influence on the development of the education and health services has been significant.

In most cases, voluntary organisations complement the work of statutory agencies. Despite the growth in statutory services over several decades the voluntary sector still flourishes and many new organisations have been established within the past few decades.

There is, of course, great diversity within the voluntary sector in relation to the aims, resources, scope of activity and type of personnel. Some employ full-time paid staff, others rely on unpaid volunteers and some have a combination of full-time staff and volunteers. Some rely solely on voluntary contributions from the public but the majority receive some statutory grants. Some focus on a particular client group such as the elderly, while others cater for a variety of groups. Some are national organisations with branches throughout the country while others have a more narrow geographic base.

Faughnan has produced a classification framework for voluntary organisations which reflects diversity in relation to dominant functions.[36] Her classification is as follows:

- *Mutual support and self-help organisations:* These are based on a common interest or need. An example is GROW, the community health movement, which has over sixty groups that meet on a regular basis.
- *Local development associations:* These associations operate within a particular geographic locality and are concerned with promoting the development of that area by collective action. The South Inner City Community Development Association in Dublin established in 1982 is an example of an association engaged in a wide range of activities.
- *Resource and service providing organisations:* According to Faughnan, these organisations represent the largest

category of voluntary activity in Ireland judged by most criteria, e.g. the largest arena for volunteer involvement. It is also the category with the greatest diversity. These organisations operate either at a local or national level. The largest organisation of this kind is the Society of St Vincent de Paul with approximately 1,100 conferences (branches) throughout the country and 10,000 members. While the main focus of the Society is on support for low income families it provides a wide range of services, including sheltered housing for the elderly and holiday homes for children.

- *Representative and coordinating organisations:* These organisations act in some cases as coordinating bodies or, more commonly, as resource agents for affiliated members of a particular category of voluntary activity and as a focal point for liaising with government or government agencies in order to bring about policy changes. Even here there is also diversity in relation to the functions and mode of operation between these representative organisations. The Disability Federation of Ireland (see p. 159) has over forty organisations affiliated to it and its general objective is to promote the welfare of the handicapped.

- *Campaigning bodies:* Many of the representatives of service organisations are also involved in campaigning for improvement in services. In practice there are few organisations whose sole function is to lobby for change. The National Campaign for the Homeless, representing a variety of voluntary organisations, was established to influence and monitor policy in relation to the homeless.

- *Funding organisations:* Within the past decade or so a number of funds or trusts have been established to support the activities and projects of voluntary organisations. These include the Ireland Funds, the Irish Youth Foundation, and the People in Need Trust. In many instances, the grants (frequently of a once-off nature) given by these organisations supplement the financial assistance provided by statutory bodies.

Evolution of voluntary activity
Faughnan has identified three main strands which influenced the development of the voluntary sector in Ireland.

Firstly, as already noted, the contribution of religious orders, commencing in the nineteenth century following Catholic emancipation, has been significant especially in the health services and education. In addition, philanthropic individuals were responsible for the establishment of voluntary hospitals in the nineteenth century. Apart from establishing voluntary hospitals, religious orders were preeminent in the field of residential care for the mentally handicapped and deprived children. Secondly, a strong community self-help tradition with a base in rural Ireland emerged in the present century. A notable example of this was Muintir na Tíre, a community based movement established in the 1930s which sought improvement in all aspects of community life. Thirdly, the development of statutory services especially those of health boards in the 1970s provided a focal point for voluntary activity. The establishment of community care programmes under health boards provided the impetus to a greater focus for voluntary organisations operating in the general welfare area, e.g. organisations providing services for the elderly and deprived children. In 1971 the Minister for Health, Erskine Childers, established the National Social Service Council with a broad remit as the focal point for voluntary social services. The NSSC helped to promote the establishment of social service councils (local coordinating bodies) throughout the country. Having been restructured in 1981 as the National Social Service Board and given a statutory basis in 1984, the Board's functions were limited to the development of information services in 1988 following an abortive attempt by the government to disband it.

Continued relevance of voluntary organisations
Paradoxically, as the role of state services has increased, that of the voluntary sector has not diminished; it has in fact also increased. Among the reasons for this are the following:

• The general pattern has been that voluntary organisations have pioneered the provision of services, with the state becoming involved in a supportive role at a later stage. The pioneering role remains relevant as new social problems emerge and as others are redefined.

- Even if it were desirable it is highly unlikely that the state could afford to completely replace the work of voluntary organisations. In many instances voluntary organisations supplement the basic services provided by the state.
- Voluntary activity provides an outlet for the altruism of many people.
- It is generally recognised that voluntary organisations can respond to social need in a more flexible manner than statutory agencies.

While the voluntary sector has obvious strengths, one of the inherent weaknesses of the system is that there may be an uneven geographic spread of organisations. While some areas may be relatively well served by voluntary groups, others may be less so. This applies in particular to services for handicapped persons where the voluntary sector has played a preeminent role. A further weakness is the lack of accountability, financial or general, in many cases.

Funding of voluntary organisations
Depending on the type of activity engaged in, there are different sources of funding for voluntary organisations. These include the European Social Fund and National Lottery funding. The main source of recurrent funds for the majority of voluntary organisations providing welfare services, however, is health boards. Section 65 of the 1953 Health Act provides that health authorities may support organisations providing services 'similar or ancillary' to those of the health authority. These Section 65 grants are in effect discretionary and there are no established criteria or guidelines for such grants. In practice, therefore, consider-able variation exists in relation to the level of funding provided. A further complicating factor is that some of the organisations are funded directly by the Department of Health – although this is mainly confined to national organisations or large organisations in the mental handicap area. The balance of funding required by voluntary organi-sations is raised in a variety of ways from the public.

Statutory/voluntary relationships
Despite its significant, if unquantifiable role in the pro-vision of services it is surprising that there is no clear policy

framework in which the voluntary sector can develop. There is a need for a broad plan which spells out the role of voluntary services in the total provision of welfare services.

In 1976 the Minister for Health, Brendan Corish, indicated that a policy document on the scope and structure of welfare services and the respective roles and relationships of the statutory and voluntary organisations in the planning and provision of these services would be prepared.[37] No such document emerged.

The short-lived Fine Gael/Labour coalition government of June 1981 to March 1982 had in its programme a commitment to introduce a charter for voluntary services which would provide a framework for the relationship between the statutory and voluntary agencies.[38] Nothing became of this charter following the change of government in March 1982 or the return of a Fine Gael/Labour government in December 1982.

It was against this background that the National Social Service Board produced a discussion document on voluntary social services in Ireland.[39] This called for an integrated approach to the development of welfare services with statutory and voluntary bodies working together. It referred to the need for greater consultation and planning between both types of agencies at local, community care area, and health board level. It suggested, for example, that the director of community care should meet with representatives of voluntary bodies in the area at least annually. At these meetings information could be exchanged on needs and services and some indication of the level of funding available could also be discussed. The document also referred to the unsatisfactory nature of funding under Section 65 grants and recommended that guidelines be established as to what type of activity would be funded, for how long and subject to what conditions.

The *Programme for Economic and Social Progress* (1991) stated that, having regard to the contribution which voluntary organisations make in delivering services and combatting poverty, the government would draw up a charter for voluntary social services. This would set out a clear framework for partnership between the state and voluntary activity and develop a cohesive strategy for supporting voluntary activity. It also indicated that a White Paper outlining the government's proposals in this area would be prepared.[40] In May 1991 the Minister for Social Welfare, Michael Woods, initiated a process of consultation with voluntary organisations in relation to the proposed charter.

Notes

Chapter 1: Introduction
1. NESC Report No. 8, *An Approach to Social Policy* (Dublin, Stationery Office, 1975), p. 30.
2. NESC Report No. 61, *Irish Social Policies: Priorities for Future Development* (Dublin, Stationery Office, 1981), pp. 12-30.
3. F. Kennedy, *Public Social Expenditure in Ireland* (Dublin, Economic and Social Research Institute, 1975), pp. 54-8.
4. NESC Report No. 61, op. cit., pp. 15-20.
5. *Building on Reality* (Dublin, Stationery Office, 1984), pp. 87-8.
6. A. Coughlan, *Aims of Social Policy* (Dublin, Tuairim Pamphlet, No. 14, 1966), p. 4.
7. See J. Higgins, *States of Welfare: Comparative Analysis in Social Policy* (Oxford, Basil Blackwell and Martin Robertson, 1981), chapter 4.
8. F. Kennedy, op. cit., pp. 11-20.
9. NESC Report No. 89, *A Strategy for the Nineties: Economic Stability and Structural Change* (Dublin, Stationery Office, 1990), p. 6.
10. S. O'Connor, *A Troubled Sky: Reflections on the Irish Educational Scene 1957-1968* (Dublin, Education Research Centre, St Patrick's College, 1986), pp. 152-3.
11. *Social Security Benefits: Northern Ireland and Republic of Ireland* (Dublin, Department of Social Welfare, 1991), p. 2.

Chapter 2: Income Maintenance
1. See D. Farley, *Social Insurance and Social Assistance in Ireland* (Dublin, Institute of Public Administration, 1964); *Report of the Commission on Social Welfare* (Dublin, Stationery Office, 1986), chapter 2.
2. See S. Ó Cinnéide, *A Law for the Poor* (Dublin, Institute of Public Administration, 1970).
3. Quoted in P. Kaim-Caudle, *Comparative Social Policy and Social Security: A Ten Country Study* (London, Martin Robertson, 1973), p. 167.

4. *Dáil Debate*, vol. 92, 23 November 1943.
5. *Building on Reality* (Dublin, Stationery Office, 1984), p. 105.
6. *Social Security* (Dublin, Stationery Office, 1949), p. 37.
7. *Budget 1975* (Dublin, Stationery Office, 1975), p. 23.
8. Farley, op. cit., p. 71.
9. *Report of the Commission on Social Welfare*, Table 21.3, p. 409.
10. *Relate*, vol. 9, no. 4 (1982), p. 4.
11. *Report of the Commission on Social Welfare*, pp. 193-4.
12. *Dáil Debate*, 20 June 1986.
13. *Programme for Economic and Social Progress* (Dublin, Stationery Office, 1991), p. 22.
14. P. Townsend, 'Poverty as Relative Deprivation: Resources and Style of Living', in D. Wedderburn (ed.), *Poverty, Inequality and Class Structure* (Cambridge, Cambridge University Press, 1974), p. 15; see also P. Townsend, *Poverty in the United Kingdom: A Survey of Household Resources and Standards of Living* (Harmondsworth, Middlesex, Penguin Books, 1979), p. 31.
15. *Poverty and the Social Welfare System* (Dublin, Combat Poverty Agency, 1988); T. Callan, B. Nolan, *et al.*, *Poverty, Income and Welfare in Ireland* (Dublin, Economic and Social Research Institute, 1989), Research Paper No. 146.
16. NESC Report No. 89, *A Strategy for the Nineties: Economic Stability and Structural Change* (Dublin, Stationery Office, 1990), pp. 222-5.
17. A. Sinfield, 'We the People and They the Poor: Comparative View of Poverty Research', *Social Studies*, vol. 4, no. 1 (1975), pp. 3-9.
18. S. Ó Cinnéide, 'The Extent of Poverty in Ireland', *Social Studies*, vol. 1, no. 4 (1972), pp. 281-400.
19. All the conference papers were published in *Social Studies*, vol. 1, no. 4 (1972). A second conference on poverty was held in Kilkenny in 1974 and the papers are published in *Social Studies*, vol. 4, no. 1 (1975). A third conference was also organised by the Council for Social Welfare, held in Kilkenny in 1981, and the papers were published in *Conference on Poverty, 1981* (Dublin, Council for Social Welfare, 1982).
20. See S. Ó Cinnéide, 'Poverty and Policy: North and South', *Administration*, vol. 33, no. 3 (1985), pp. 378-412.
21. Ibid., p. 393.
22. Combat Poverty Agency, *Strategic Plan* (Dublin, Combat Poverty Agency, 1987), p. 2.

Chapter 3: Housing

1. Department of the Environment, *A Plan for Social Housing* (Department of the Environment, 1991), p. 1. This contains the most recent statement but similar objectives were

outlined, for example, in the White Paper *Housing in the Seventies* (Dublin, Stationery Office, 1969) p. 3.

2. There are two county councils in Tipperary, North Riding and South Riding.

3. This section contains a summary of developments up to the mid-1960s as outlined by P.J. Meghan, *Housing in Ireland* (Dublin, Institute of Public Administration, 1966).

4. *Economic Development* (Dublin, Stationery Office, 1959), p. 46.

5. F. Kennedy, *Public Social Expenditure in Ireland* (Dublin, Economic and Social Research Institute, 1975), p. 15.

6. NESC Report No.14, *Population Projections 1971-86: The Implications for Social Planning – Dwelling Needs* (Dublin, Stationery Office, 1976); NESC Report No. 69, *Housing Requirements and Population Change 1981-91* (Dublin, Stationery Office, 1983).

7. T. Corcoran, 'Government Policies towards Public Housing' in J. Blackwell (ed.), *Towards an Efficient and Equitable Housing Policy* (Dublin, Institute of Public Administration, 1989).

8. See NESC Report No. 87, *A Review of Housing Policy* (Dublin, Stationery Office, 1989), where the pros and cons of local authority purchase schemes are outlined, pp. 177-81.

9. P. Tansey, 'Housing Subsidies: A Case for Reform' in J. Blackwell (ed.), op. cit., pp. 31-2.

10. *A Plan for Social Housing*, p. 6.

11. P. Pfretzschner, *The Dynamics of Irish Housing* (Dublin, Institute of Public Administration, 1965), p. 112.

12. B. Harvey and M. Higgins, 'The Links between Housing and Homelessness' in J. Blackwell (ed.), op. cit., p. 36.

13. L. O'Brien and B. Dillon, *Private Rented: The Forgotten Sector* (Dublin, Threshold, 1982).

14. *Programme for Economic and Social Progress* (Dublin, Stationery Office, 1991), p. 37.

15. For background, see *A Plan for Social Housing*, pp. 28-33.

16. B. Thompson, 'Social Housing' in J. Blackwell and S. Kennedy (eds.), *Focus on Homelessness* (Dublin, Columba Press, 1988), pp. 118-9.

17. *Programme for Economic and Social Progress*, p. 36.

18. *A Plan for Social Housing*, p. 15.

19. Statistics used in this section are taken from the *Census of Population*.

20. NESC Report No. 87, op. cit., p. 28.

21. NESC Report No. 23, *Report on Housing Subsidies* (Dublin, Stationery Office, 1977), pp. 8-11.

22. T.J. Baker and L.M. O'Brien, *The Irish Housing System: A Critical Overview* (Dublin, Economic and Social Research Institute, 1979).

23. J. Blackwell, 'Do Housing Subsidies Show a Redistribution to

the Poor?' in *Conference on Poverty, 1981* (Dublin, Council for Social Welfare, 1982), pp. 225-8.

24. NESC Report No. 89, *A Strategy for the Nineties: Economic Stability and Structural Change* (Dublin, Stationery Office, 1990), p. 238.

Chapter 4: Education

1. There are many excellent works dealing with the development of first level education and the education system in general. One of the most recent is J. Coolahan, *Irish Education: History and Structure* (Dublin, Institute of Public Administration, 1981). Other works include: D.H. Akenson, *The Irish Education Experiment* (London, Routledge and Kegan Paul, 1970), which deals with the national system of education in the nineteenth century; N. Atkinson, *Irish Education, a History of Education Institutions* (Dublin, Hodges Figges, 1969); P.J. Dowling, *A History of Irish Education* (Cork, Mercier Press, 1971); F.S.L. Lyons, *Ireland Since the Famine* (London, Fontana, 1973) (relevant sections); J.J. Lee, *The Modernisation of Irish Society, 1848-1919* (Dublin, Gill and Macmillan, 1973), chapter 1; T.J. McElligot, *Education in Ireland* (Dublin, Institute of Public Administration, 1966).

2. See P.J. Dowling, *The Hedge Schools of Ireland* (Cork, Mercier Press, 1968).

3. D.H. Akenson, op. cit., chapter 1.

4. *Report of the Primary Education Review Body* (Dublin, Stationery Office, 1990), p. 93.

5. *The Irish Times,* 21 October 1974.

6. *Report of the Primary Education Review Body,* p. 36.

7. *Investment in Education* (Dublin, Stationery Office, 1965), pp. 225-66.

8. NESC Report No. 19, *Rural Areas; Social Planning Problems* (Dublin, Stationery Office, 1976), pp. 52-3.

9. *The Irish Times,* 8 February 1977.

10. *Rules for National Schools under the Department of Education* (Dublin, Stationery Office, 1965), p. 8.

11. *Programme for Action in Education, 1984-1987* (Dublin, Stationery Office, 1984), p. 16.

12. The block grant is calculated by reference to a complex formula which takes account of the number of day pupils and boarding pupils in Protestant schools.

13. *Investment in Education,* p. 150.

14. S. O'Connor, *A Troubled Sky: Reflections on the Irish Educational Scene, 1957-1968* (Dublin, Educational Research Centre, St Patrick's College, 1986), p. 193.

15. *Department of Education School Transport Scheme,* Report of

Study carried out by Hyland Associates Ltd (Dublin, Stationery Office, 1979).

16. C. Murphy, 'School Transport Levy not to be Introduced – Wilson', *The Irish Times*, 21 June 1979.

17. J.H. Whyte, *Church and State in Modern Ireland, 1923-1970* (Dublin, Gill and Macmillan, 1971), p. 38.

18. Coolahan, op. cit., p. 103.

19. G. Hussey, *At the Cutting Edge: Cabinet Diaries 1982-1987* (Dublin, Gill and Macmillan, 1990), p. 128.

20. *Investment in Education*, pp. 154-68.

21. *Review of National Policies for Education: Ireland* (Paris, OECD, 1969), appendix iv, p. 122.

22. Ibid., p. 129.

23. *Partners in Education* (Dublin, Stationery Office, 1985), p. 10.

24. *Review of National Policies for Education: Ireland*, pp. 124-5.

25. Steering Committee on Technical Education, *Report to the Minister for Education on Regional Technical Colleges* (Dublin, Stationery Office, 1969).

26. Lyons, op. cit., p. 93.

27. *Commission on Higher Education, 1960-67, vol. 1, Presentation and Summary of Report* (Dublin, Stationery Office, 1967), p. 49.

28. Ibid., p. 50.

29. *Higher Education Authority, Reports, Acounts (1989) and Students' Statistics, 1988-89* (Dublin, Higher Education Authority, 1991), p. 15.

30. *Commission on Higher Education*, vol. 2, pp. 760-63.

31. P. Clancy, *Who Goes to College? A Second National Survey of Participants in Higher Education* (Dublin, Higher Education Authority, 1988), p. 28.

32. A.D. Tussing, 'Accountability, Rationalisation and the White Paper on Educational Development', in 'Symposium on White Paper on Education', *Journal of the Statistical and Social Inquiry Society of Ireland*, vol. xxiv, part 3, 1980-81, p. 76.

33. Higher Education Authority, *General Report 1974-1984* (Dublin, Stationery Office, 1985), p. 77. See also P. Clancy, 'The Evolution of Policy in Third Level Education', in D.G. Mulcahy and D. O'Sullivan (eds.), *Irish Educational Policy: Process and Substance* (Dublin, Institute of Public Administration, 1989), pp. 112-14.

34. *Adult Education in Ireland* (Dublin, Stationery Office, 1973).

35. *Lifelong Learning: Report of the Commission on Adult Education* (Dublin, Stationery Office, 1984), p. 9.

36. M. Bassett, B. Brady, T. Fleming and T. Inglis, *For Adults Only: A Case for Adult Education in Ireland* (Dublin, Aontas, National Association of Adult Education, 1989), p. 44.

37. P. Clancy and C. Benson, *Higher Education in Dublin: A Study of Some Emerging Needs* (Dublin, Higher Education Authority, 1979), pp. 13-16.
38. P. Clancy, *Participation in Higher Education: A National Survey* (Dublin, Higher Education Authority, 1982).
39. P. Clancy, (1988), op. cit.
40. *Report of the Primary Education Review Body*, p. 103.
41. A.D. Tussing, 'Equity and the Financing of Education', in S. Kennedy (ed.), *One Million Poor?* (Dublin, Turoe Press, 1981), p. 211.
42. *Programme for Economic and Social Progress* (Dublin, Stationery Office, 1991), p. 31.
43. S. O'Connor, op. cit., chapter 1.
44. A.D. Tussing (1980-81), op. cit., p. 71.
45. *Programme for Economic and Social Progress*, pp. 33-4.

Chapter 5: Health Services

1. R. Barrington, *Health, Medicine and Politics in Ireland, 1900-1970* (Dublin, Institute of Public Administration, 1987), p. 279.
2. There are various accounts of the controversy surrounding the Mother and Child Scheme. These include relevant sections in Barrington, op. cit.; N. Browne, *Against the Tide* (Dublin, Gill and Macmillan, 1986); J. Deeny, *To Cure and to Care: Memoirs of a Chief Medical Officer* (Dublin, Glendale Press, 1989); J.H. Whyte, *Church and State in Modern Ireland, 1923-1979*, 2nd edn (Dublin, Gill and Macmillan, 1980).
3. B. Hensey, *The Health Services of Ireland*, 4th edn (Dublin, Institute of Public Administration, 1988).
4. *The Health Services and their Further Development* (Dublin, Stationery Office, 1966) pp. 6-64.
5. The National Health Council was established under the Health Act of 1953 to advise the Minister for Health on such matters affecting, or incidental to, the health of the people as may be referred to it by the Minister and on such other general matters (other than conditions of employment of officers and servants and the amount or payments of grants and allowances) relating to the operation of the health service as it thinks fit.
6. Department of Health, *Health: The Wider Dimensions* (Department of Health, 1986), p. 35.
7. Barrington, op. cit., p. 284.
8. NESC Report No. 84, *Community Care Services: An Overview* (Dublin, Stationery Office, 1987), pp. 5-6.
9. *The Health Services and their Further Development*, p. 30.
10. *The General Practitioner in Ireland – Report of the Consultative*

Council on General Medical Services (Dublin, Stationery Office, 1974), p. 45.

11. *Report of the Working Party on Prescribing and Dispensing in the General Medical Service* (Dublin, Stationery Office, 1976), p. 45.

12. *Report of the Working Party on the General Medical Service* (Dublin, Stationery Office, 1984).

13. *The Future Organisation of General Practice in Ireland: A Discussion Document* (Dublin, Irish College of General Practitioners, 1986), p. 34.

14. *Report of the Commission on Health Funding* (Dublin, Stationery Office, 1989), p. 218.

15. NESC Report No. 84, op. cit., chapter 6.

16. *Outline of the Future Hospitals System – Report of the Consultative Council on the General Hospital Service* (Dublin, Stationery Office, 1968).

17. *The Irish Times*, 21 October 1975.

18. *Action Plan for National Reconstruction*, Fianna Fáil Manifesto for General Election, 1977, p. 25.

19. Comhairle na nOspidéal, *2nd Report January 1975 – December 1978* (Dublin, 1978), p. 24.

20. P. McQuillan, 'What Should we Provide? Service Emphasis to Achieve Objectives'. Paper presented at Conference on Health in the 1990s (Association of Health Boards in Ireland in association with the Institute of Public Administration, 1987), pp. 55-6.

21. *Report of the Commission of Inquiry on Mental Illness* (Dublin, Stationery Office, 1966), p. xv.

22. *The Irish Psychiatric Hospital Census, 1981* (Dublin, Medico-Social Research Board, 1983), pp. 11-12.

23. *The Psychiatric Services: Planning for the Future* (Dublin, Stationery Office, 1984).

24. *Report of the Commission on Health Funding*, p. 365.

25. *Green Paper on Mental Health* (Dublin, Stationery Office, 1992) p. 14.

26. *Report of the Commission of Inquiry on Mental Handicap* (Dublin, Stationery Office, 1965).

27. *Programme for Social and Economic Progress* (Dublin, Stationery Office, 1991), p. 28.

28. *Report of the Commission on Health Funding*, p. 15.

29. L. Joyce and C. Ham, 'Enabling Managers to Manage: Health Care Reform in Ireland', *Administration*, vol. 38, no. 3 (1990), p. 227.

30. NESC Report No. 89, *A Strategy for the Nineties: Economic Stability and Structural Change* (Dublin, Stationery Office, 1990), pp. 285-6.

31. *Health Services News*, vol. 2, no. 2, May 1990, pp. 4-5.

32. Address by Dr Rory O'Hanlon, TD, Minister for Health, at the launch of the Report of the Dublin Hospital Initiative Group and the announcement of the reorganisation of health services, 18 September 1991.

Chapter 6: Welfare Services

1. *The Care of the Aged* (Dublin, Stationery Office, 1968), p. 13.
2. *Report of the Commission on Social Welfare* (Dublin, Stationery Office, 1986), p. 191.
3. N. Fogarty, L. Ryan and J. Lee, *Irish Values and Attitudes* (Dublin, Dominican Press, 1984), p. 25.
4. *The Years Ahead: A Policy for the Elderly* (Dublin, Stationery Office, 1988), p. 19.
5. See, for example, Rent Tribunal, *Annual Report and Accounts, 1985* (Dublin, Stationery Office, 1985), p. 8.
6. *The Years Ahead*, p. 24.
7. *Report on the Industrial and Reformatory Schools System* (Dublin, Stationery Office, 1970), p. 6.
8. See R. Gilligan, *Irish Child Care Services – Policy, Practice and Provision* (Dublin, Institute of Public Administration, 1991).
9. *Towards a Full Life: Green Paper on Services for Disabled People* (Dublin, Stationery Office, 1984), p. 18.
10. Ibid., p. 21.
11. NESC Report No. 50, *Major Issues in Planning Services for Mentally and Physically Handicapped Persons* (Dublin, Stationery Office, 1980), p. 12.
12. *Report of the Primary Education Review Body* (Dublin, Stationery Office, 1990), p. 60.
13. *Training and Employing the Handicapped: Report of a Working Party established by the Minister for Health* (Dublin, Stationery Office, 1975), preface.
14. The figure had not risen above 1.4 per cent. See *Annual Report of the National Rehabilitation Board, 1989*.
15. NESC Report No. 84, *Community Care Services: An Overview* (Dublin, Stationery Office, 1987), chapter 5.
16. NESC Report No. 50, op. cit., p. 15.
17. *Towards a Full Life*, pp. 72-3.
18. *Report of the Commission on Social Welfare*, chapter 19.
19. *Towards a Full Life*, p. 112.
20. *Response to the Green Paper on Services for Disabled People* (Dublin, Union of Voluntary Organisations for the Handicapped, 1985), pp. 31-2.
21. D.B. Rottman, A.D. Tussing and M.M. Wiley, *The Population Structure and Living Circumstances of Irish Travellers: Results from the 1981 Census of Traveller Families* (Dublin, Economic and Social Research Institute, 1986), p. 73.

22. *Report of the Commission on Itinerancy* (Dublin, Stationery Office, 1963), pp. 12-13.
23. *Report of the Travelling People Review Body* (Dublin, Stationery Office, 1983), pp. 5-6.
24. *Report of the Commission on Itinerancy*, pp. 34-5.
25. *The Travellers' Health Status Study: Vital Statistics of Travelling People, 1987* (Dublin, Health Research Board, 1989), p. 24.
26. *Report of the Commission on Itinerancy*, p. 64.
27. *Report of the Travelling People Review Body*, pp. 59-60.
28. Committee to Monitor the Implementation of Government Policy on Travelling People, *Fifth Report*, 1989, pp. 14-17.
29. *Report of the Travelling People Review Body*, pp. 81-2.
30. *Report of the Commission on Itinerancy*, p. 61.
31. *Report of the Travelling People Review Body*, p. 38.
32. Committee to Monitor the Implementation of Government Policy on Travelling People, op. cit., p. 3.
33. *Report of the Travelling People Review Body*, op. cit., p. 35.
34. Under the Prohibition of Incitement to Racial, Religious or National Hatred Act of 1989, the travelling people are cited as a group about whom offensive material cannot be published.
35. S.B. Gmelch, 'From Poverty Sub-culture to Political Lobby: The Traveller Rights Movement in Ireland', in C. Curtin and T.M. Wilson (eds.), *Ireland from Below: Social Change and Rural Communities* (Galway, Galway University Press, 1990).
36. P. Faughnan, *Partners in Progress: Voluntary Organisations in the Social Service Field* (Dublin, 1990), section 1.
37. *Dáil Debates*, 29 April 1976.
38. Fine Gael-Labour, *Programme for Government, 1981-86.*
39. *The Development of Voluntary Social Services in Ireland: A Discussion Document* (Dublin, National Social Service Board, 1982).
40. *Programme for Economic and Social Progress* (Dublin, Stationery Office, 1991), p. 24.

Bibliography

General

Building on Reality, Dublin, Stationery Office, 1984

Burke, H., *The People Under the Poor Law in 19th Century Ireland*, Dublin, The Women's Education Bureau, 1987

Coughlan, A., *Aims of Social Policy*, Dublin, Tuairim Pamphlet, 1966

Kaim-Caudle, P., *Social Policy in the Irish Republic*, London, Routledge & Kegan Paul, 1967

Kearney, C.P., *Selectivity Issues in Irish Social Services*, Dublin, Family Study Centre, University College Dublin, 1991

Kennedy, F., *Public Social Expenditure in Ireland*, Dublin, Economic and Social Research Institute, 1975

NESC Report No. 8, *An Approach to Social Policy*, Dublin, Stationery Office, 1975

NESC Report No. 61, *Irish Social Policies: Priorities for Future Development*, Dublin, Stationery Office, 1981

NESC Report No. 89, *A Strategy for the Nineties: Economic Stability and Structural Change*, Dublin, Stationery Office, 1990

Programme for Economic and Social Progress, Dublin, Stationery Office, 1991

White, J.H., *Church and State in Modern Ireland, 1923-1979*, 2nd edn, Dublin, Gill & Macmillan, 1980

Income Maintenance

Callan, T., B. Nolan *et al.*, *Poverty, Income and Welfare in Ireland*, Dublin, Economic and Social Research Institute, 1989

Council for Social Welfare, *Emerging Trends in the Social Welfare System?*, Dublin, Council for Social Welfare, 1992

Farrelly, D., *Social Insurance and Social Assistance in Ireland*, Dublin, Institute of Public Administration, 1964

Ó Cinnéide, S., *A Law for the Poor*, Dublin, Institute of Public Administration, 1970

Ó Cinnéide, S., 'The Extent of Poverty in Ireland', *Social Studies*, vol. 1, no. 4 (1972)

Ó Cinnéide, S., 'Poverty and Policy: North and South', *Administration,* vol. 33, no. 3 (1985)

Poverty and the Social Welfare System, Dublin, Combat Poverty Agency, 1988

Report of the Commission on Social Welfare, Dublin, Stationery Office, 1986

Report of the Review Group on the Treatment of Households in the Social Welfare Code, Dublin, Stationery Office, 1991

Reports of the Department of Social Welfare, Dublin, Stationery Office

Reynolds, B. and S.J., Healy (eds.), *Poverty and Family Income Policy,* Dublin, Conference of Major Religious Superiors, 1988

Housing

Baker, T.J. and L.M. O'Brien, *The Irish Housing System: A Critical Overview,* Dublin, Economic and Social Research Institute, 1979

Blackwell, J., 'Do Housing Subsidies Show a Redistribution to the Poor?' in *Conference on Poverty, 1981,* Dublin, Council for Social Welfare, 1982

Blackwell, J. (ed.), *Towards an Efficient and Equitable Housing Policy,* Dublin, Institute of Public Administration, 1989

Blackwell, J. and S. Kennedy (eds.), *Focus on Homelessness,* Dublin, Columba Press, 1988

Department of the Environment, *Annual Housing Statistics*

Department of the Environment, *A Plan for Social Housing,* Dublin, Department of the Environment, 1991

NESC Report No. 23, *Report on Housing Subsidies,* Dublin, Stationery Office, 1977

NESC Report No. 87, A *Review of Housing Policy,* Dublin, Stationery Office, 1989

O'Brien, L. and B. Dillon, *Private Rented: The Forgotten Sector,* Dublin, Threshold, 1982

Education

Bassett, M., B. Brady, T. Fleming and T. Inglis, *For Adults Only: A Case for Adult Education in Ireland,* Dublin, Aontas, National Association of Adult Education, 1989

Coolahan, J., *Irish Education: History and Structure,* Dublin, Institute of Public Administration, 1981

Clancy, P., *Participation in Higher Education: A National Survey,* Dublin, Higher Education Authority, 1982

Clancy, P., *Who Goes to College? A Second National Survey of Participants in Higher Education,* Dublin, Higher Education Authority, 1988

Clancy, P. and C. Benson, *Higher Education in Dublin: A Study of Some Emerging Needs,* Dublin, Higher Education Authority, 1979

Commission on Higher Education 1960-67, Dublin, Stationery Office, 1967

Department of Education, *Statistical Reports*

Education for a Changing World, Dublin, Stationery Office, 1992

Investment in Education, Dublin, Stationery Office, 1965

Lifelong Learning: Report of the Commission on Adult Education, Dublin, Stationery Office, 1984

Mulcahy, D.G. and D. O'Sullivan (eds.), *Irish Educational Policy: Process and Substance*, Dublin, Institute of Public Administration, 1989

O'Connor, S., *A Troubled Sky: Reflections on the Irish Educational Scene, 1957-1968*, Dublin, Education Research Centre, St Patrick's College, 1986

Partners in Education, Dublin, Stationery Office, 1985

Programme for Action in Education 1984-1987, Dublin, Stationery Office, 1984

Report of the Primary Education Review Body, Dublin, Stationery Office, 1990

Reports of the Department of Education, Dublin, Stationery Office

Tussing, A.D., *Irish Educational Expenditures – Past, Present and Future*, Dublin, Economic and Social Research Institute, 1978

Tussing, A.D., 'Accountability, Rationalisation and the White Paper on Educational Development' in 'Symposium on White Paper on Education', *Journal of the Statistical and Social Inquiry Society of Ireland*, vol. xxiv, part 3, 1980-81

Health Services

Barrington, R., *Health, Medicine and Politics in Ireland 1900-1970*, Dublin, Institute of Public Administration, 1987

Department of Health, *Health Statistics*, Dublin, Stationery Office

Department of Health, *Health: The Wider Dimensions*, Department of Health, 1986

Green Paper on Mental Health, Dublin, Stationery Office, 1992

The Health Services and their Further Development, Dublin, Stationery Office, 1966

Hensey, B., *The Health Services of Ireland*, 4th edn, Dublin, Institute of Public Administration, 1988

NESC Report No. 84, *Community Care Services: An Overview*, Dublin, Stationery Office, 1987

Outline of the Future Hospitals System – Report of the Consultative Council on the General Hospital Service, Dublin, Stationery Office, 1968

The Psychiatric Services: Planning for the Future, Dublin, Stationery Office, 1984

Report of the Commission on Health Funding, Dublin, Stationery Office, 1989

Report of the Working Party on the General Medical Service, Dublin, Stationery Office, 1984

Reports of the General Medical Services (Payments) Board

Welfare Services

The Care of the Aged, Dublin, Stationery Office, 1968

The Development of Voluntary Social Services in Ireland: A Discussion Document, Dublin, National Social Service Board, 1982

Faughnan, P., *Partners in Progress: Voluntary Organisations in the Social Service Field,* Dublin, 1990

Gilligan, R., *Irish Child Care Services – Policy, Practice and Provision,* Dublin, Institute of Public Administration, 1991

NESC Report No. 50, *Major Issues in Planning Services for Mentally and Physically Handicapped Persons,* Dublin, Stationery Office, 1980

Report of the Commission on Itinerancy, Dublin, Stationery Office, 1963

Report on the Industrial and Reformatory Schools System, Dublin, Stationery Office, 1970

Report of the Task Force on Child Care Services, Dublin, Stationery Office, 1980

Report of the Travelling People Review Body, Dublin, Stationery Office, 1983

Reports of the Committee to Monitor the Implementation of Government Policy on Travelling People

Rottman, D.B., A.D. Tussing and M.M. Wiley, *The Population Structure and Living Circumstances of Irish Travellers: Results from the 1981 Census of Traveller Families,* Dublin, Economic and Social Research Institute, 1986

Towards a Full Life: Green Paper on Services for Disabled People, Dublin, Stationery Office, 1984

Training and Employing the Handicapped: Report of a Working Party established by the Minister for Health, Dublin, Stationery Office, 1975

The Years Ahead: A Policy for the Elderly, Dublin, Stationery Office, 1988

Index